Laurina's Kitchen

GENERATIONS OF HEIRLOOM DISHES FROM THE ECOBELLI FAMILY

**LORA LEE ECOBELLI
& TOM ECOBELLI**

SQUARE CIRCLE PRESS
VOORHEESVILLE, NEW YORK

Laurina's Kitchen:
Generations of Heirloom Dishes From the Ecobelli Family

Published by
Square Circle Press LLC
137 Ketcham Road
Voorheesville, NY 12186
www.squarecirclepress.com

© 2012 by Lora Lee Ecobelli and Tom Ecobelli.
All rights reserved. No part of this publication may be reproduced or transmitted in any form or by any means, electronic or mechanical, except brief quotes extracted for the purpose of book reviews or similar articles, without permission in writing from the publisher.

First paperback edition 2012.
Printed and bound in the United States of America on acid-free, durable paper.

ISBN 13: 978-0-9833897-9-8
ISBN 10: 0-9833897-9-9
Library of Congress Control Number: 2012943731

Publisher's Acknowledgments

Cover design © 2012, Richard Vang, Square Circle Press. All images courtesy of the authors, unless otherwise noted in text. "Lena", from *Kitchen Tales*, courtesy of Lora Lee Ecobelli.

Authors' Acknowledgments

The authors wish to thank Don Rittner of the Schenectady County Film Commission for his enthusiasm for this book and for introducing us to the publisher; Ann Hauprich of Legacies Unlimited for her support and tireless publicity work for both this book and our movie project; book contributors who prepared recipes and/or provided photos: Frank Rebco, Adira Amram and Bram Muller, Laure-Jeanne Davignon, Elizabeth Breslin, Carolyn Cocca and Jenny Quirk, Steve and Diane O'Connor, Alana Amram, David Amram, Adam Amram, Chelsea Lauber and Boo Boo Kitty, Peter Marino, and Phyllis Hoeck; all the family, former restaurant staff and customers who contributed memories and stories; and Richard Vang of Square Circle Press, who gathered all these ingredients together, poured them into the mold of our idea, and created a memorable dish.

To our friends and family,

former employees, and everyone else

who made Ecobelli's Tam O'Shanter Inn

a part of their lives for so many years.

Thank You

Laurina's Kitchen

INTRODUCTION
A NOTE FROM THE PUBLISHER	0.04
WELCOME TO THE ECOBELLI FAMILY	0.05
LAURINA & HER KITCHEN	0.07

ECOBELLI'S A LA CARTE

Menus	0.02
"The Tam"	0.16
Inside "the Tam"	0.24
"Coat of Arms" Logo	0.30
Waitresses & Staff	0.40
"Tramp" the Dog	0.53
"Babs" & the Bar	0.56
Family Sampler	0.78
Ecobelli's At Large	0.86
Restaurant Reviews	0.88

SALADS & APPETIZERS
ANTIPASTO	0.10
MAZZIE	0.11
EGGPLANT CAPONATA	0.12
HOLIDAY SEAFOOD SALAD	0.13
CLAMS CASINO	0.14
STUFFED ARTICHOKES	0.15

SOUPS
ITALIAN WEDDING SOUP	0.18
PASTA FAGIOLI	0.20
MINESTRONE	0.21
CHICKPEA SOUP	0.22
MINESTRA	0.23

PIZZA PIE
PIZZA MEMORIES	0.26
PIZZA PIE	0.27
ASSEMBLING THE PIZZA	0.28
GARLIC KNOTS	0.29

PASTA SAUCES
A SAUCE OF PRIDE	0.32
"LENA"	0.33
SPAGHETTI SAUCE	0.34
MEATBALLS	0.35
MARINARA SAUCE	0.36
BOLOGNESE SAUCE	0.37
PUTTANESCA SAUCE	0.38
SPAGHETTI CARUSO	0.39

Menu

PASTA DISHES

FRESH EGG PASTA & RAVIOLI DOUGH	0.44
WATER GLASS RAVIOLI	0.45
LAURINA'S FAMOUS LASAGNA	0.46
EGGPLANT PARMIGIANA	0.47
ZITI SICILIAN	0.48

SEAFOOD

MUSSELS MARINARA	0.50
SHRIMP FRA DIAVOLO	0.51
ZUPPA DE PESCA	0.52
SHRIMP WITH PEAS AND PIMIENTOS	0.54
LINGUINE WITH WHITE CLAM SAUCE	0.55

FAMILY SPECIALS

Tom's Olives	0.70
Alana's Southern Italian Sweet Potatoes	0.72
David's La Boheme Survival Omelet	0.73
Bramram's Ravioli w/ Sage Butter	0.74
Adam's Octopus	0.76
Leo's Buried Chicken	0.77

MEAT DISHES

BRACIOLE	0.58
ITALIAN OVEN FRIED CHICKEN	0.59
MADEIRA	0.60
CHICKEN CACCIATORE	0.61
PICATA	0.62
SCALLOPINO	0.63
CHICKEN ROMANO	0.64
BREADED CUTLETS & PARMIGIANA	0.65
ROSEMARY CHICKEN	0.66
EASTER LAMB	0.67
ROAST CHICKEN AND SAUSAGE	0.68

DESSERTS

AUNT ANNA'S CHRISTMAS COOKIES	0.80
LEMON ICE	0.81
PIGNOLI COOKIES	0.82
LEMON RICOTTA EASTER PIE	0.83
AMARETTO CHEESECAKE	0.84
E-WANDS	0.85

CUSTOMER COMMENTS

RESTAURANT REVIEWS	0.88
STAFF MEMORIES	0.89
WORD OF MOUTH	0.92

TAKE-OUT MENU

ABOUT THE AUTHORS: LORA LEE ECOBELLI	0.98
ABOUT THE AUTHORS: TOM ECOBELLI	0.99
CHICKADEE: THE MOVIE	1.00

Laurina's Kitchen

Ecobelli's Menus

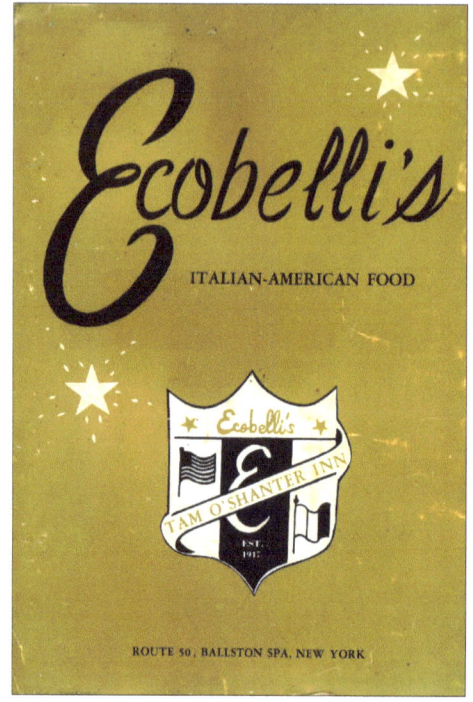
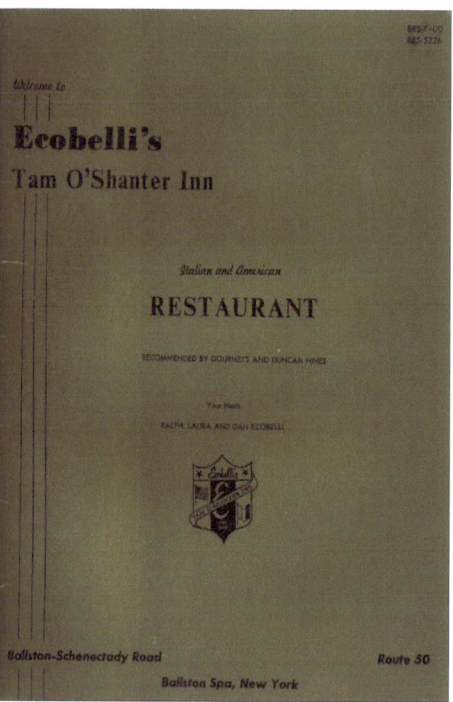

A selection of covers showing the evolution of the Ecobelli's menu from a "folksy" image to one of a fine dining establishment. Though hard to read at this size, the wording on the menu cover changed from "Italian-American" to "Italian and American," reflective of the expansion of the menu to include standard American fare along with traditional Italian dishes. Also of note is the mention on later menus that the restaurant was recommended by both *Gourmet* magazine and food critic Duncan Hines. By the time the red menu was presented, Ecobelli's had solidified its reputation and such promotional text was no longer necessary. At right is a detail of the cocktail list from the menu on the opposite page.

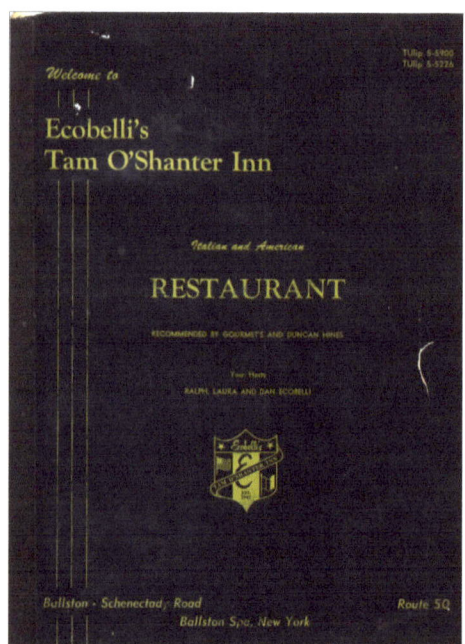
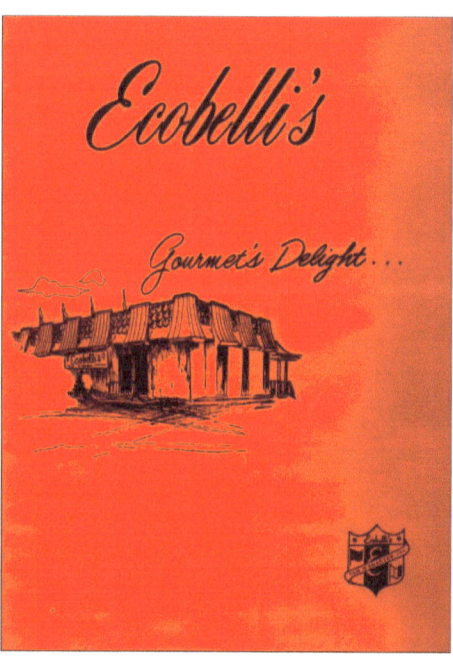

Cocktails

GRASSHOPPER	.85
PINK SQUIRREL	.85
TAM O'SHANTER SPECIAL	.70
Sherry and Dubonnet Wine	
ALEXANDER	.85
Gin, Creme de Cocoa	
ALEXANDER	.90
Brandy, Creme de Cocoa	
BACARDI	.80
Rum, Grenadine, Lemon	
COFFEE COCKTAIL	.85
Port Wine, Brandy Egg and Sugar	
CUBA LIBRE	.80
Rum, Coca Cola, Lime	
DAIQUIRI - PLAIN	.80
Rum, Sugar, Lime	
DUBONNET	.80
Dubonnet Wine, Gin	
GIN RICKEY	.75
Gin, Lime, Vichy	
JOHN COLLINS	.75
Whiskey, Lemon, Vichy	
SOUTHERN COMFORT MANHATTAN	.85
So. Comfort & Imported Sw. Vermouth	
OLD FASHIONED	.85
Whiskey, Bitters, Sugar, Fruit	
PINK LADY	.85
Gin, Lime, Grenadine, Egg White	
SLOE GIN FIZZ	.80
Sloe Gin, Lemon, Sugar, Vichy	
TOM COLLINS	.80
Gin, Lemon, Sugar, Vichy	
WARD EIGHT	.80
Whiskey, Lemon, Grenadine, Vichy	
ROB ROY	.90
Scotch with Imported Vermouth	
SIDE CAR	.85
Brandy, Cointreau, Lemon	
SINGAPORE SLING	.85
Gin, Lemon, Sugar, Cherry, Brandy, Fruit	
ORANGE BLOSSOM	.75
Gin, Orange Juice, Sugar	

INTRODUCTION

A NOTE FROM THE PUBLISHER	0.04
WELCOME TO THE ECOBELLI FAMILY	0.05
LAURINA & HER KITCHEN	0.07

A full spread from the vintage Ecobelli's menu shown at top left on the opposite page.

A Note from the Publisher

IN DECEMBER OF 2011 Don Rittner, Schenectady County Film Commissioner, contacted me about a film project and asked if I would be interested in publishing the companion cookbook. He put me in touch with Lora Lee and Tom Ecobelli, the brother and sister team who co-wrote both the movie, *Chickadee*, and this cookbook. After discussing their book project with them, I knew right away that I wanted to publish it. I had been looking for a cookbook manuscript for Square Circle Press for some time, but I didn't want to publish a typical cookbook. From their manuscript and their presentation, I could see that Ecobelli's wasn't just a restaurant, but rather it had been an Upstate New York institution. This, coupled with their grandmother Laurina's personal story outlined in their movie project, indicated to me that this was indeed something extraordinary, and that it fit well into our publishing mission of upstate history and culture.

While there used to be many more than there are today, Upstate New York was once dotted with family-run Italian restaurants, and you could find one in almost every sizable village or city. Though many that still exist have gone through modernizations and new ownership, there are some that retain their original charm, both architecturally and socially. A few that come to my mind that I have dined in are Moretti's in Elmira, Petta's in Schenectady, Parillo's in Amsterdam, and Lombardo's in Albany.

My own Italian restaurant memories are of Sorge's Restaurant in my hometown of Corning. I remember various family celebrations there, and the dark wooden booths that ran parallel to the lunch counter where generations of Crystal City residents have eaten. Although the restaurant recently burned and was refurbished, the food is still the same as I remember, and I still go there when I can for a small plate of spaghetti and red sauce, topped with a meatball and a sausage. When I think of Italian food, I think of Sorge's.

Lora Lee and Tom possessed an enormous amount of material from their family's restaurant — photos, menus, memorabilia — and memories. But because Ecobelli's was a regional icon, we knew there had to more out there, and, with the help of Ann Hauprich, we engaged in a publicity campaign to solicit and obtain more materials from the public at large. The response was overwhelming, for such memories of the food from places like Ecobelli's and Sorge's are extremely difficult to erase from one's mind. These restaurants are deeply embedded within the culture — and the very psyche — of Upstate New York and its people.

It took a good deal of time to collect, organize, and compile all the materials into this book, and, as any foodie knows, a good presentation is important. The inspiration for the design and layout of this book came directly from the vintage Ecobelli's menu shown on the previous page. I loved its retro style and typesetting, and holding it in my hands provided a feeling of nostalgia that I wanted to capture — including some of the "homemade" or "amateurish" charm of the printing and design.

Many of the images do not bear captions. While some speak for themselves, other do not, and as anyone who has tried to research their family history knows, often times a generation will pass before the historical information is shared, and is sometimes lost. Anyone with more information about a photo is invited to contact the authors and share what they know.

The family recipes were passed down orally to Lora Lee and Tom, so those former customers still around who are looking to duplicate the exact Ecobelli taste that they remember are encouraged to experiment with the recipes, and we wish you success. But what we know *will* satisfy them is this big, heaping plate of memories.

Richard Vang
Square Circle Press

Welcome to the Ecobelli Family

I LEARNED TO COOK by watching my grandmother Laurina in our restaurant kitchen. Some of my earliest memories are of falling asleep there in a bread box beside her. As young as five years old I was given a job to do. It might have been as simple as peeling carrots, but I learned from my grandmother's gentle and artful ways. Italian food needs to be made lovingly from scratch. If you want great lasagna you have to make great sauce first. You should always use fresh ingredients whenever possible. Free range chicken and organic meats are always the best choice. Not only are they healthier, the taste is beyond comparison and you will feel better about helping the environment. We always had a big garden growing up and fresh herbs and vegetables were readily available. By growing our own vegetables it just made us appreciate a good meal even more. In our family, recipes were hardly ever written down, but we all cooked together and learned by example. At the end of the day we all sat down to a meal together, and I believe that despite some very hard times, it is what held us all together.

Most of the recipes in this book have been handed down through the generations. Some are my own, but each one of those I chose to include are heavily influenced by what the great cooks in our family taught me. Laurina learned from her mother and then down the line. Cooking together was the heart and soul of who we were. As soon as my own children were old enough to walk I had them in the kitchen with me and they all have become quite accomplished. I truly believe that a family who shares a meal together is a healthy family. ~ Lora Lee

I'M NOT A QUARTER OF THE CHEF my sister is or my other relatives were, but what I do have is a good cook's instincts stamped into my DNA. It's hard to explain, but if you have those instincts, you always know the right seasoning a dish needs, how much is too much, how much is too little. You have a feeling when something is cooked to perfection. You know when it's time to take the item off the stove or out of the oven no matter what the recipe reads. You have a sixth sense that kicks in just before something burns or a pot boils over. You're not afraid to mix items most people would never dream of combining, but something in you knows it will work … and it usually does. I like to believe this is part of the legacy my family left me. I know I think of at least one of them every time I cook, even if I'm just throwing something quick in the microwave. The crackle, the pop, the sizzle of food is all somehow connected to the laughing, tears and sensations of my memories.

Our family not only expressed their love with what they put on your plate, but other emotions, such as jealousy, longing, friendship, loneliness, or even courage. For a long time I worried about mixing emotions like that with food. Why couldn't we express such feelings in other ways? Luckily, I let go of trying to figure out the mystery. What difference does it make? Over time, what sunk into my consciousness was the single most driving force in their lives: the love they held in their hearts for all of us. That's the message I hold on to. Besides, life is lot more fun if it tastes good! ~ Tom

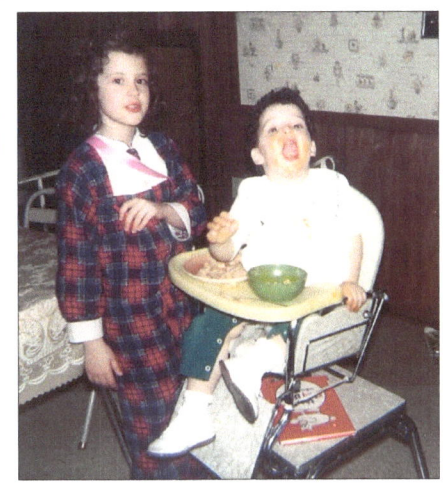

Our family rarely told us exactly how much of any ingredient went into their dishes, just, "a little of this, a little of that …" That's why you'll see written "to taste" so often. We want you to feel free to modify these dishes to suit your own taste buds. Don't be afraid to experiment. In doing so, you'll see how each dish will become unique to you, your family and your kitchen. ~ Lora Lee & Tom

Clockwise, from top left: Laurina, age 14; Donato and Laurina's wedding, 1923; Donato holding Raphelo; Laurina and her three children, Joanne, Clementine and Raphelo; Laurina, Donato, Clementine and Raphelo pose for a family portrait; Clem and her husband Tony Merola; Ralph, Laura and Dan, as they were known at the restaurant; (center) Ralph and Clem with Dan and Laura at the couple's 50th wedding anniversary dinner.

   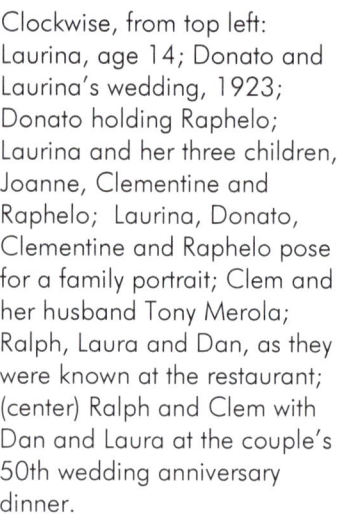

Laurina & Her Kitchen

LAURINA INZINNA WAS BORN in the United States in 1906. Her parents, Michelina and Salvatore, had emigrated to America from Collesano, Sicily. While Laurina was still an infant, Salvatore died, leaving the family destitute. Laurina and her older sister Elizabeth were placed into the Mother Cabrini Catholic Orphanage in Hoboken, New Jersey. After several years Michelina remarried and was able to reclaim her children. Her new husband moved the family to upstate New York to work in the textile mills. Unfortunately, Laurina's stepfather became increasingly abusive and Laurina found herself the center of a landmark domestic violence trial. Drawing upon an inner strength beyond her years, Laurina bravely defied the odds and brought her abusive stepfather to justice. (More information about this incident in Laurina's life and the movie *Chickadee* is presented on page 100.)

Our grandfather Donata (Dan) Ecobelli was from a little town in Italy called Benevento. He was a merchant seaman who traveled the world and was an excellent musician who played many instruments. In 1923 he married our grandmother, Laurina (Laura) Inzinna. They lived in Hoboken, New Jersey while raising their two children Raphelo (Ralph) and Clementine (Clem). In Hoboken our grandfather ran a small shoe shop until the Mafia, then called The Black Hand, threatened him if he did not give them protection money. When he refused, they threw a molotov cocktail through the shop window, burning it to the ground. Left with nothing, my grandfather went off to sea with the merchant marines and Laurina went to work in a sweat shop in New York City.

When our father, Ralph Ecobelli, returned from the service in 1946, the family decided to return to upstate New York, where Laurina's sister had been running Sam Pepe's restaurant in Amsterdam. Our grandparents began looking for a place of their own, and in 1947, somehow managed to scrape together enough money to buy a rundown Scottish tavern in Ballston Spa called The Tam O'Shanter Inn. "The Tam," as it was known in town, was the favorite watering hole of down-and-out bookies and gamblers heading to the Saratoga Race Track. Our grandfather was superstitious after his exchange with The Black Hand and decided not to change the name. Hence it was forever called, "Ecobelli's Tam O'Shanter Inn." It was a strange mix and a mouthful to say, but no one seemed to mind.

Knowing nothing about the tavern business, our family dove in head first. Our grandfather, being a very gregarious person, tended bar and entertained customers with his mandolin playing and lively stories. Our father, his sister Clem, and her husband Tony pitched in as a team and did whatever needed to be done. When Laurina cooked meals for the family in the tiny back kitchen, she always shared whatever it was with the tavern customers and it wasn't long before word spread about her delicious food. In a matter of months the roadside pub had become the most popular place to be.

Our father Ralph partnered with his parents and became an accomplished chef. He took over cooking duties in the evening and Laurina worked the day shift. Soon they expanded the tavern into a full blown restaurant. They really had no choice, since crowds of townspeople were filling the tiny tavern to capacity every night.

Over the years, the little tavern grew and grew. An enlarged kitchen, banquet center, and second story were added in the '50s and '60s, and the staff expanded to over 40 workers, consisting of aunts, uncles, cousins, and various neighborhood kids who needed a job. Many loyal employees stayed with our family for over 30 years. Everyone was treated like family and each night before work, our grandmother prepared a sit-down dinner for the entire staff so they could share a meal. To reward the employees for their hard work and loyalty, our father implemented a profit-sharing plan, one of the first in the area.

Not only was "The Tam" known for excellent home-cooked food, but also its warm and friendly atmosphere. Laurina's generosity was legendary. She fed numerous families over the years that were going through hard times and they never forgot her acts of kindness. To this day, generations of people remember her and the "The Tam" fondly as a favorite place for special occasions and holiday dinners.

Together with their children and extended family, Laurina and Dan had transformed the local Scottish tavern into one of the region's premier and most popular Italian restaurants. Ecobelli's Tam O'Shanter Inn was written up by *Gourmet* magazine, Golden Press Cookbook, and Duncan Hines, as well as several local and regional publications. It was also a charter member of World Famous Restaurants International and a member of the National Restaurant Association of America.

Laurina and Dan traveled extensively in Italy and Europe, and along with the traditional recipes that they already knew, they incorporated some of the recipes that they found on their travels into the menu and made them their own.

Eventually, Ralph took over as president and chef and with his unique twists on Laurina's original recipes, the restaurant continued to grow. Ralph employed such innovations as a "non-smokers" night, restaurant gift certificates, and a series of radio spots and newspaper ads featuring staff — and long-time, loyal customers — with their photos, bios and favorite Ecobelli dishes. Dan passed away, and as Laurina grew older she slowed down a bit, but she still prepared her signature dishes and remained a vital part of the ongoing day-to-day operations.

The business was sold in 1979 to Joe and Tony Iaia, a pair of brothers in the restaurant business in Schenectady, but our family retained a lifetime of friends and memories. Our father retired, but Laurina continued to do prep work for the new owners, including making a huge pot of minestra every Wednesday as a weekly special for the customers still loyal to her and her delicious food. She wasn't getting paid. She just couldn't resist helping out. That truly exemplifies who she was.

Laurina passed away in 1981, but her legacy lives on. She remains famous not only for her recipes, but even more for her hospitality, her generosity, and service to her community.

SALADS & APPETIZERS

ANTIPASTO	0.10
MAZZIE	0.11
EGGPLANT CAPONATA	0.12
HOLIDAY SEAFOOD SALAD	0.13
CLAMS CASINO	0.14
STUFFED ARTICHOKES	0.15

Salads

1967		1968	
Sat July 29	235	Sat July 27	210
Tues Aug 1	181	Tues " 30	194
Wed " 2	165	Wed " 31	199
Thurs " 3	222	Thurs Aug 1	158
Fri " 4	223	Fri " 2	230
Sat " 5	275	Sat " 3	246
	1301		1237
Tues " 8	198	Tues " 6	187
Wed " 9	181	Wed " 7	151
Thurs " 10	193	Thurs " 8	174
Fri " 11	231	Fri " 9	247
Sat " 12	304	Sat " 10	313
	1107		1072
Tues " 15	228	Tues " 13	199
Wed " 16	231	Wed " 14	194
Thurs " 17	205	Thurs " 15	184
Fri " 18	255	Fri " 16	258
Sat " 19	325	Sat " 17	268
	1244		1103

This document recording the number of salads prepared gives an idea of the restaurant's volume in its heyday.

Antipasto

SALAD INGREDIENTS

SALAD GREENS
  Romaine lettuce, escarole, endive, arugula, radicchio, endive, fresh basil, dandelion, water cress
VEGETABLES
  Tomato, radish, fennel, celery heart, carrot, cucumber, red onion, Italian olive, artichoke heart, heart of palm, pepperoncini, white mushroom, portobello mushroom, red and yellow pepper, zucchini, eggplant, chickpea, stuffed grape leaf
MEATS
  Salami, capicolla, prosciutto, pepperoni, anchovy
CHEESES
  Crumbled Gorgonzola, Provolone, fresh or smoked mozzarella

PREPARED BY Lora Lee Ecobelli Saugerties, NY

PHOTO BY Richard Vang Knox, NY

LORA LEE'S DRESSING

OLIVE OIL, extra virgin	3/4 cup
LEMON JUICE, fresh squeezed	1 lemon
RED WINE VINEGAR	1 splash
DIJON MUSTARD	1 tbsp
WORCESTERSHIRE SAUCE	1 splash
CAPERS	1 tbsp
SHALLOTS or GARLIC, minced	1 tsp
OREGANO, dried or fresh	1/2 tsp
KOSHER SALT	1 tsp
BLACK PEPPER, fresh ground	to taste

Start with a peppery blend of salad greens mixed with crisp romaine lettuce. After you have arranged your salad greens on a large platter, you're ready to get creative. You can use any or all of the ingredients suggested above; it's really a dish suited to your tastes. Try combinations of raw, pickled, marinated, roasted, or grilled veggies, they all work well. And remember, the presentation is almost as important as the flavors, so have fun!

For the freshly made dressing, whisk all the ingredients together until the dressing is smooth and creamy. You can prepare this early and use the dressing to marinate the raw fresh mushrooms, grilled vegetables and roasted peppers. Pour over the antipasto just before serving.

In an Italian meal, the antipasto is the first course and a real labor of love, an artful display of salad greens, vegetables, cheeses and meats. There is no set rule on how to assemble this magnificent salad but here is your chance to show off all your artistic abilities. I made huge festive platters of it for my daughter Adira's wedding and it was devoured within minutes. As my grandmother Laurina said, "A good antipasto always brings people together."

My grandfather would take me with him every spring when he went digging for the very best, tender, young dandelion greens he could find for the antipasto. Many times I worried we might be arrested while trespassing on private property, but he seemed to relish the danger. Dandelions are too bitter to be used any other time than early spring, so don't dig up your yard in August or you'll be sorely disappointed. ~ Lora Lee

Mazzie

One of my earliest jobs in the restaurant was to help assemble the antipastos with the ancient salad prep Mazzie. I'm sure she wasn't always old, but to my memory she was a bent-over woman of about eighty-five who worked very slowly — but her antipastos were a sight to behold. Even at the young age of five, I knew I was learning from a true master. Mazzie had worked for my family since they opened the restaurant in 1947 and took great pride in her creations. Each salad was uniquely made for the individual tastes of her customers. I would sit up on the counter and watch her work. But the most unpleasant job was left up to me. I had to stick my fingers into the anchovy tins and pull out the tiny fish because Mazzie's arthritic fingers could no longer grasp them. As much as I adore antipasto I'm still not a fan of anchovies because of that slimy memory!
~ Lora Lee

Mazzie, at center, with other Ecobelli's staff (see page 40).

As a kid I would assist Mazzie with making salads too, but I was kind of afraid of her because she was all business, no play. Her head would bob in concentration as she made sure each radish, celery stalk, olive and tomato were placed just right. Every Christmas as a gift, she would bake us a box of amazing Christmas cookies, including Rice Krispies treats, years before they were popular. She lived in a cute little cottage not far from the restaurant that looked just like a gingerbread house. ~ Tom

Laurina enjoying the beach with family and friends.

Eggplant Caponata

INGREDIENTS

OLIVE OIL, extra virgin	1/2 cup
SPANISH ONION, chopped, 1/2 inch dice	1 large
RED BELL PEPPER, chopped	1
GARLIC, chopped fine	4 cloves
EGGPLANT, cut, 1/2 inch cubes	4 cups
SALT	to taste
BLACK PEPPER, fresh ground	to taste
TOMATO PASTE	1 (6 oz) can
TOMATOES, diced	1 (12 oz) can
KALAMATA OLIVES, chopped fine	1/2 cup
CAPERS	2 tbsp
BALSAMIC VINEGAR	1/3 cup
OREGANO, dried	1/2 tsp
SUGAR	2 tbsp
PARSLEY, chopped (for garnish)	

ITALIAN BREAD ROUNDS, toasted

PREPARED BY Lora Lee Ecobelli Saugerties, NY

PHOTO BY Lora Lee Ecobelli Saugerties, NY

Heat a large sauté pan over medium heat and add a splash of olive oil. Add the onion, red bell pepper and garlic, and sauté until tender. Add the eggplant (peel it first if you prefer), salt and pepper to taste, and cook until nicely browned and softened. Add the tomato paste, diced tomatoes, olives, capers, balsamic vinegar, oregano and sugar.

Bring the mixture to a boil then lower the heat and let the liquid reduce. Adjust the seasoning to your taste. Remove from heat and cool. Refrigerate overnight to let flavors marinate.

Before serving bring caponata to room temperature and garnish with chopped parsley. To serve, spoon onto toasted Italian bread rounds. Caponata holds one week in the refrigerator or up to 6 months in the freezer — but it will probably get eaten long before then!

Laurina's brother (center) and buddies during World War II.

Holiday Seafood Salad

INGREDIENTS

WHITE WINE	1 cup
GARLIC, whole	2 cloves
BAY LEAF	1
THYME, dried	1/2 tsp
SHRIMP, large, cleaned, deveined	1 lb
BAY SCALLOPS	1 lb
CALAMARI with tentacles, cleaned, sliced into rings	1 lb
OLIVE OIL, extra virgin	6 tbsps
GARLIC, minced	2 cloves
SALT	to taste
BLACK PEPPER, fresh ground	to taste
KALAMATA OLIVES, pitted, halved	1/2 cup
LEMON JUICE, fresh squeezed	1 lemon
LEMON PEEL, shaved	1 tsp
ITALIAN PARSLEY, fresh, chopped	2 tbsps
CELERY, chopped	2 ribs
SCUNGILLI, rinsed, sliced*	1 lb

PREPARED BY
Tom Ecobelli
Los Angeles, CA

PHOTO BY
Tom Ecobelli
Los Angeles, CA

*If you cannot get fresh scungilli, you can often find it canned or frozen, or under the name of conch. One 12-ounce can will work.

In a small stockpot add the wine, whole garlic, bay leaf and thyme. Add the shrimp, scallops and calamari to poach, about 5 minutes or until shrimp turns pink. Do not overcook. Remove seafood from liquid, drain, let cool, and set aside.

In a large bowl mix the olive oil, minced garlic, salt, pepper, olives, lemon juice, shaved lemon peel, parsley and celery. Add the scungilli and cooled seafood. Toss evenly to coat. Let the entire dish marinate in the refrigerator for 1 hour, but it is best if it is left overnight.

Prepping the Christmas Eve fish dinner for the restaurant was a huge task. Friends, family, and even the occasional customer pitched in. It all tasted great when it made it to the table, but as a little kid I was more fascinated with the live snails, eels and fresh fish as they were delivered, before they made it to the oven. I was awed watching Laurina expertly debone a flounder with a knife she allowed me to sharpen (carefully). I was proud when the other grownups couldn't shuck oysters and clams with the lightning twist of the wrist my father could. But the most fun was taking the mountain of trimmings outside to our barn cats. Watching them enjoy their feast as much as we enjoyed ours was the best. ~ Tom

Laurina and Tom, Christmas, c. 1967.

Clams Casino

INGREDIENTS

BACON	5 strips
GARLIC, minced	3 cloves
CELERY, chopped fine	1 rib
RED BELL PEPPER, chopped fine	1/2 pepper
ONION, chopped fine	1 small
PARMIGIANO CHEESE, grated	1/4 cup
BREAD CRUMBS	2 cups
CRUSHED RED PEPPER FLAKES (to taste)	1/2 tsp
OREGANO, dried or fresh	1/2 tsp
PARSLEY, fresh, chopped fine	2 tsps
SALT	1 tsp
BLACK PEPPER, fresh ground fine	1/2 tsp
OLIVE OIL, extra virgin	1/2 cup
LEMON PEEL, grated	1 tsp
LEMON JUICE, fresh squeezed	1/2 cup
CLAMS, Cherrystone or Littleneck	3 doz

PREPARED BY Lora Lee Ecobelli Saugerties, NY

PHOTO BY Lora Lee Ecobelli Saugerties, NY

Fry the bacon until crisp, remove it from the pan and chop finely. Drain off most of the bacon fat, reserving some in the pan. In the remaining fat, sauté the garlic, celery, red bell pepper and onion until tender. Do not brown.

In a medium-size bowl mix the cheese, bread crumbs, red pepper flakes, oregano, parsley, salt and pepper together. Add the sautéed vegetables, bacon, olive oil, lemon peel and lemon juice. Stir all together to form a crumbly mixture.

Scrub the clams and open them carefully, placing them on a baking pan. To loosen the clam from its shell, just slide your knife under the clam meat to sever it. Sprinkle each lightly with lemon juice, and pack tightly with the bread crumb mixture. Drizzle each with more olive oil. Broil about 5 minutes, until the stuffing is bubbly and golden brown.

Our restaurant was a family-owned business and everyone put in long hours. The only day off was Monday, and that was the day my father would scout out what other restaurants were doing. We would all pile into the car and he would easily drive five hours to some hole-in-the-wall that he had heard made good scaloppini. Dad was a good businessman and knew he needed to understand his competition. For someone who never studied the culinary arts he was a pretty innovative chef for the times. He was constantly creative, developing new dishes or expanding existing ones.

One of his favorite places he would take us was a little mom-and-pop restaurant in Schenectady called Cornell's. We went there for their amazing Clams Casino. With their permission my dad added their recipe to his menu, enhanced of course by his own special twist, but he was always careful to credit the originator. They were really delicious and I myself could eat a dozen! ~ Lora Lee

I remember that when I was little, I would refuse to eat the clams, but I loved to eat the stuffing. Finally, I took the plunge, gobbled one down, and never looked back. ~ Tom

Stuffed Artichokes

INGREDIENTS

ARTICHOKES	6 large
LEMON JUICE, fresh squeezed	1 cup
OLIVE OIL, extra virgin (more if needed)	1 cup
SALT	to taste
BLACK PEPPER, fresh ground	to taste
GARLIC, cloves, slivered	1 bulb
GARLIC, chopped	2 tbsps
BREAD CRUMBS	2 cups
GRATED CHEESE	
Parmigiano, Romano, or Asiago	1/2 cup
OREGANO, dried or fresh	1/2 tsp
WATER (more if needed)	1/4 cup

PREPARED BY Tom Ecobelli, Los Angeles, CA

PHOTO BY Tom Ecobelli, Los Angeles, CA

Look for the plumpest, greenest artichokes you can find. Make sure they are firm and clear of any brown discoloration. With a sharp serrated knife, cut off the tops and bottoms. Using a pair of kitchen shears, clip the ends of the exterior leaves. Sprinkle with lemon juice to prevent discoloration and set aside.

Oil the bottom of a heavy-bottomed pan, Dutch oven, or large ceramic baking pan. Loosen the leaves of the artichokes so you can easily fill them with stuffing. Sprinkle with the salt and pepper. Liberally insert the slivered garlic deep into the cavities between the leaves and set aside. In a medium-sized bowl, mix the chopped garlic, bread crumbs, grated cheese, oregano, 1/2 cup of the lemon juice, and 1/2 cup of the olive oil. The mixture should have a crumbly texture.

With a teaspoon, insert the stuffing into the cavities between the leaves. Fill tightly and drizzle with more olive oil. Place the stuffed artichokes in the pan and fill the bottom with 1/4 cup water, 1/4 cup of the lemon juice, 2 tablespoons of the olive oil, salt and pepper. You will use this liquid to baste the artichokes, but it evaporates quickly so you may need to add more water. Bake at 350° for about 1 hour, basting occasionally.

The artichokes are done when you can easily pull off the leaves and the stuffing is brown. Serve them at room temperature with a slice of lemon.

Artichokes are an Italian delicacy and are always served on holidays, especially Easter. They take a lot of work to prepare but the payoff is worth it when you see your family smile as you bring them to the table. ~ Lora Lee

Ecobelli's Tam O'Shanter Inn

From an Ecobelli's menu: "You may wonder how an Italian restaurant has a connection with a Scotch (not Irish) name. It's rather simple: when the Ecobelli's took over in 1947, the Tam O' Shanter was built and operated by a Scotch family. It was known throughout the area as "the Tam" and we were unknown, originally coming from New Jersey. We thought we would change it in time after we became established. After 20 years it's still the same due to the fact that it has become a novelty to many of our customers to see an Italian association with a Scotch name. We haven't seen where it has hindered us; therefore we have kept the "Tam O'Shanter" and it has been good to us."

SOUPS

ITALIAN WEDDING SOUP	0.18
PASTA FAGIOLI	0.20
MINESTRONE	0.21
CHICKPEA SOUP	0.22
MINESTRA	0.23

YOU'D NEVER RECOGNIZE IT NOW, but this is the way the Tam O'Shanter Inn on Route 50 south of Ballston Spa looked when the Ecobelli family purchased it on January 15, 1947. The structure has undergone five separate periods of renovations in the ensuing 32 years, increasing its customer capacity from 60 to 270 people. Through the dedicated efforst of the Ecobelli family, the little business grew from supporting its original staff of four to a full complement of forty in 1978. The old fireplace seen on the exterior of the original structure now may be seen in the front interior wall of the restaurant's dining room. The fifth and final period of renovation took place in 1972.

Italian Wedding Soup

SOUP STOCK

CHICKEN, medium size, whole	1
WATER	4 quarts
CARROTS, whole	4
CELERY, chopped	2 cups
ONION, large, whole	1
GARLIC, chopped	5 cloves
PARSLEY, fresh, chopped	1/2 cup
KOSHER SALT	to taste
BLACK PEPPER, fresh ground	to taste
ESCAROLE, chopped rough	1 head
ORZO pasta	1/2 cup

PREPARED BY
Tom Ecobelli
Los Angeles, CA

PHOTO BY
Tom Ecobelli
Los Angeles, CA

CHICKEN MEATBALLS

CHICKEN, ground	1 lb
BREAD CRUMBS	1/2 cup
EGG	1
ROMANO CHEESE, grated	1/4 cup
KOSHER SALT	1 tsp
BLACK PEPPER, fresh ground	1 tsp
OREGANO, dried	1/2 tsp
GARLIC, chopped fine	2 cloves
PARSLEY, dried	1/2 tsp

This delicious rich chicken soup takes a long time to prepare but it's worth the wait. It was always served on holidays as a special treat. ~ Lora Lee

EGG DROP MIXTURE

EGGS, beaten	2
KOSHER SALT	to taste
BLACK PEPPER, fresh ground	to taste
ROMANO CHEESE, grated (more for garnish)	2 tsps
PARSLEY, dried (more for garnish)	1/2 tsp

Ralph and Mary Ecobelli pose for their wedding portrait, 1955.

Cover the whole chicken with water in a large stock pot. Add carrots, celery, onion, garlic, parsley, salt and pepper. Simmer on low for about 1 1/2 hours, or until the chicken falls off the bones. Remove the chicken, carrots and onion, and let the stock cool. Discard the onion. After the stock has cooled, skim the fat off the top with a spoon and discard. Pick the meat from the bones, being careful to remove all the skin and fat. Shred the meat, mash the whole carrots, and return both to the stock. Taste test the stock for seasoning. Add salt and pepper if needed. Bring heat of the stock back up to a low simmer.

While the stock is heating, make the chicken meatballs. In a medium-size bowl, add the ground chicken, bread crumbs, egg, Romano cheese, salt, pepper, oregano, garlic and parsley. Use your hands to mix, and roll into nickel-size balls (they will double in size). Drop the meatballs into the hot soup. Add the chopped escarole and cook for about 45 minutes more. Raise the heat to high, add the Orzo pasta, and bring to a rolling boil.

Beat the eggs and sprinkle with the salt, pepper, Romano cheese and parsley. When the soup reaches a nice rolling boil, add the egg drop mixture. Do not stir the soup until the eggs are set. Once you see long strings and clumps of the egg drops, stir well to mix them nicely into the soup.

Serve soup immediately with more Romano cheese sprinkled on top. Make sure you save the leftovers. The soup will be even better the next day!

Ralph and Mary's wedding party, Schenectady, NY, 1955.

Pasta Fagioli

INGREDIENTS

CANNELLINI BEANS, dry	3 cups
OLIVE OIL, extra-virgin	2 tbsps
PANCETTA or BACON, chopped	3 slices
ROSEMARY, fresh, whole	2 sprigs
THYME, fresh, whole	1 sprig
BAY LEAVES, dried (or 1 large fresh)	2
ONION, chopped	1 medium
CARROTS, chopped	2
CELERY, chopped	3 ribs
GARLIC, large, chopped	5 cloves
KOSHER SALT	to taste
BLACK PEPPER, fresh ground	to taste
TOMATOES, crushed	1 (16 oz) can
WATER	2 cups
CHICKEN STOCK	2 quarts
DITALINI pasta	1-1/2 cups

GARLIC BREAD ROUNDS, toasted, sprinkled with grated PARMESAN CHEESE

PREPARED BY
Lora Lee Ecobelli
Saugerties, NY

PHOTO BY
Lora Lee Ecobelli
Saugerties, NY

Soak the beans overnight. Drain and rinse.

Heat a heavy stock pot over medium-high heat and add the olive oil and pancetta. Brown the pancetta bits lightly, and add the rosemary, thyme, bay leaf, onion, carrots, celery and garlic. Season with salt and pepper to taste. Add the beans, tomatoes, water and chicken stock. Raise the heat to high, and let boil for about 10 minutes.

Reduce the heat and simmer for 2 hours, or until the beans are tender. You may need to add additional stock as the beans will absorb the liquid. Adjust all the seasonings to taste as you go along.

After 2 hours, bring the soup back up to boil and add the pasta. Cook until the pasta is *al dente*. The leaves of the rosemary and thyme sprigs will separate from their stems as the soup cooks; remove them and discard.

When the pasta is cooked, ladle the soup into bowls and top with toasted garlic bread rounds. Sprinkle with grated Parmesan cheese and fresh ground black pepper.

This was one of our father's favorite soups. It definitely qualifies as Italian comfort food. ~ *Lora Lee*

Laurina (center) enjoying a repast with family and friends at the Amsterdam, NY home of her daughter Joanne and husband Tony D'Carlo (standing behind Laurina).

Minestrone

INGREDIENTS

OLIVE OIL, extra virgin	1/3 cup
ONION, medium, chopped	1
CARROTS, chopped small	3
CELERY, chopped	1/2 cup
GARLIC, chopped	4 cloves
GREEN BEANS, fresh, cut	1/2 cup
RED BELL PEPPER, chopped	1
ZUCCHINI, small, cubed	1
VEGETABLE BROTH	4 cups
TOMATOES, diced	1 (28 oz) can
RED KIDNEY BEANS, drained	1 (15 oz) can
CANNELLINI or GREAT NORTHERN BEANS, drained	1 (15 oz) can
PARSLEY, fresh, minced	2 tbsps
OREGANO, dried	1/2 tsp
BASIL, dried or fresh	1 tsp
WATER	2 cups
KOSHER SALT	1 tbsp
BLACK PEPPER	1/2 tsp
SHELL pasta, small	1/4 lb
ESCAROLE, chopped or KALE or SPINACH	2 cups
PARMESAN CHEESE, grated (for garnish)	

PREPARED BY
Lora Lee Ecobelli
Saugerties, NY

PHOTO BY
Lora Lee Ecobelli
Saugerties, NY

Heat the olive oil over medium heat in a large soup pot. Sauté the onions, carrots, celery, garlic, green beans, red bell pepper and zucchini until the onions begin to turn translucent. Add the vegetable broth, tomatoes, canned beans, parsley, oregano, basil, water, salt and black pepper.

Bring the soup to a boil, then reduce the heat and simmer for 30 minutes. Add the escarole, kale or spinach leaves. Add the shell pasta and cook until the pasta is *al dente*. Add more salt if needed.

To serve, sprinkle with Parmesan cheese and fresh ground pepper.

Laurina could whip this up in a flash but it always changed depending on whatever vegetables she had on hand. She could stretch it to feed a crowd, and it is another soup that keeps getting better as the days go by. ~ Lora Lee

Laurina hosting a dinner party for her brothers and sisters.

Chickpea Soup

INGREDIENTS

OLIVE OIL, extra virgin	1/3 cup
ONION, chopped	1 cup
CARROTS, chopped	3
CELERY, chopped small	1/2 cup
RED BELL PEPPER, chopped	1
GARLIC, chopped	4 cloves
BEEF or TURKEY, ground	1 lb
CRUSHED RED PEPPER FLAKES	1/2 tsp (to taste)
CHICKEN BROTH	4 cups
WATER	1 cup
CHICKPEAS, drained	1 (15 oz) can
TOMATOES, diced	1 (28 oz) can
PARSLEY, fresh, chopped	1 tbsp
OREGANO, dried	1 tsp
KOSHER SALT	1-1/2 tsps
BLACK PEPPER, fresh ground	1 tsp
SPAGHETTI, broken into 1-inch pieces	1/4 lb
PARMESAN or ROMANO CHEESE, grated (for garnish)	

PREPARED BY
Lora Lee Ecobelli
Saugerties, NY

PHOTO BY
Lora Lee Ecobelli
Saugerties, NY

Heat the olive oil over medium heat in a large soup pot. Sauté the onions, carrots, celery, red bell pepper and garlic until the onions begin to turn translucent. Add the ground meat and red pepper flakes and cook until browned.

Add the chicken broth, water, chickpeas, tomatoes, parsley, oregano, salt and pepper. Bring the soup to a boil, then reduce the heat and allow the soup to simmer for 30 minutes. Add more salt if needed. Add the spaghetti and cook until the pasta is *al dente*.

To serve, sprinkle with Parmesan or Romano cheese and fresh black pepper.

This is one of my very favorites and my children loved it growing up. It takes no time to make and it's really nutritious. I sometimes make a pot of it and eat it all week. ~ Lora Lee

Ralph (left) and his older sister Joanne (center) with friends on a night out.

Minestra

INGREDIENTS

OLIVE OIL, extra virgin	2 tbsps
PORK COUNTRY SPARE RIBS	4
ITALIAN SAUSAGE	2 links
ONION, large	1
GARLIC, sliced	4 cloves
PEPPERONI, sliced thin	6-inch chunk
CHICKEN BROTH	1 quart
WATER	2 cups
CANNELLINI BEANS	1 (24 oz) can
SALT	to taste
BLACK PEPPER, fresh ground	to taste
SAVOY CABBAGE	1 head
ESCAROLE, chopped coarse	1 head

PREPARED BY Lora Lee Ecobelli Saugerties, NY

PHOTO BY Lora Lee Ecobelli Saugerties, NY

In a heavy stock pot, brown the spare ribs and sausage in the olive oil. Add the onion and garlic and sauté until tender. Remove the sausage and slice it into bite size pieces.

Return the sausage to the pot, add the pepperoni and cook for a few more minutes to release its flavor. Add the chicken broth, water, beans, salt and pepper. Bring soup to a boil. Reduce the heat to low, then skim off the meat fat.

Add the cabbage and escarole, then cover and simmer for about 2 hours. Adjust seasonings to taste. Serve in big bowls with crusty bread for sopping up the extra soup.

In 1966 the Saratoga Performing Arts Center (SPAC) opened in Saratoga Springs and the Philadelphia Orchestra began its yearly residence there. Word spread throughout the orchestra about the little Italian restaurant in Ballston Spa that made authentic, home-style food, and we were soon flooded with hungry musicians. My grandfather, being a musician himself, was thrilled to have such enthusiastic and distinguished clientele. One patron in particular, a boisterous Italian-American bassoonist named Adelchi Louis Angelucci, became instant friends with Dan. "Angie" loved to go into the kitchen to watch Laurina cook. He always said good food was the true music of his soul. He encouraged Laurina to cater to his gastronomic fancies by bringing her boxes of chocolate. In return she made him all the delectable peasant dishes he had grown up with. Minestra was his favorite. ~ Lora Lee

Lora Lee, Clementine and Dan testing out Lora Lee's first guitar at Laurina and Dan's home, c. 1966.

Inside "the Tam"

PIZZA PIE

PIZZA MEMORIES	0.26
PIZZA PIE	0.27
ASSEMBLING THE PIZZA	0.28
GARLIC KNOTS	0.29

The dining room, just after the Ecobellis purchased the restaurant in 1947.

Pizza Memories

The Tam was known far and wide for its pizza, and generations ordered a pie every Friday night from Ecobelli's. When I moved to New York City at 18, I was appalled at the doughy, bland pizza I found there. Only when I went to visit my grandfather's birth place in Benevento, Italy did I find the sort of heavenly pizza I had grown up with: a crispy, thin-crust Neapolitan-style with spicy sauce, homemade sausage and toppings.

Our family took great pride in the ingredients they used in their pizza. Several times a week they made hundreds of pounds of homemade sausage for the pizza and other dishes. They ground all the meat and spices themselves, and on the days they were making sausage, you could smell the aroma all through the neighborhood.

I graduated to making pizzas when I was about ten. I learned the ropes from my grandmother's helpers Anna and Janet. I wasn't allowed to use the brick oven yet, but I helped to make the dough in a huge mixer that was bigger than me. Instead of play dough, I had pizza dough to play with. What more could a kid want? If there is one thing I really miss from my childhood, it is a slice of Laurina's "special" pizza with sausage, black olives, peppers and mushrooms — a taste that was truly sublime. ~ Lora Lee

I wish I had a picture of the pizza-making area. Above the big bread board in front of the pizza oven were dozens of handmade posters of all of the pizza "milestones," such as:

- New Year's Eve, 1956. We did it! 300 pizzas, by Ralph, Janet, Babs, Dan and Laura!
- September 5, 1970 - 260 pizzas by Ralph, Stephen, Janet, Anna and Babs.

Obviously the numbers increased as the years rolled on (left). These were accompanied by goofy, hand-drawn pictures and scribbled signatures. It was a testament to the teamwork and good will our father and grandparents strove to establish in spite of the heated pace in the kitchen. No matter how busy, they kept the working environment fun, supportive and fair. ~ Tom

Pizza Pie

DOUGH

ACTIVE DRY YEAST	1 (.25 oz) pkg
WATER, warm	1 cup
BREAD FLOUR, sifted	2 cups
OLIVE OIL, extra virgin	2 tbsps
SEA SALT, fine	1 tsp

(Makes three 12-inch, thin crust pizzas.)

SAUCE

TOMATOES, organic, crushed	1 (16 oz) can
GARLIC, chopped	2 cloves
SALT	1 tsp
BLACK PEPPER, fresh ground coarse	1/2 tsp
OREGANO, dried	1 tsp
BASIL, dried	1 tsp
ROSEMARY, dried	1/2 tsp
CRUSHED RED PEPPER FLAKES (optional)	1/2 tsp

IMAGE FROM Vintage Ecobelli's Restaurant Menu

PIZZA DOUGH: In a small bowl, dissolve the yeast in warm water. Let stand until creamy, about 10 minutes.

In a larger bowl, combine the flour, olive oil and salt. Make a well in the center of the flour and pour the yeast in the center. Using a spatula, draw in the ingredients, working from the outside in, and then mix with your hands to form a firm dough that pulls away from the bowl.

Knead the dough briefly on a floured work board just until it takes on more flour and is not sticking to your hands.

Place the dough in a lightly oiled bowl. Score the top on the dough and rub with a little oil to prevent cracking, and cover with a dish towel. Let the dough rise in a warm place until it doubles in size, about 1 to 2 hours.

When the dough has doubled in size, punch it down with your fist to prevent air bubbles. Place it back down on your floured work board and divide it into three sections with a pastry knife. Knead the three sections of dough into three equal size balls.

Grease three 12-inch pizza pans, then sprinkle the bottom of the pans with yellow cornmeal. (The cornmeal helps to create a crispier crust.) Place one dough ball in the center of the pan, flour your hands so they don't stick to the dough and, using your fingertips, stretch the dough, starting from the center and working your way to the edges, making sure it is evenly distributed.

When dough is stretched completely to the edges, sprinkle lightly with flour and set aside. It will continue to rise as you prepare the pizza sauce and toppings.

PIZZA SAUCE: Mix all the ingredients together. The sauce will store refrigerated for several days. (Note: the sauce ingredients are for one pie; you can triple it to match the amount of dough above, or you can freeze the extra dough to make another pie later.)

Assembling the Pizza

TOPPINGS

MEATS	your choice
VEGETABLES	your choice
PARMESAN CHEESE, shredded	to taste
ASIAGO CHEESE, shredded	to taste
MOZZARELLA CHEESE, shredded or sliced	to cover
OLIVE OIL, extra virgin	

Using a tablespoon, spread the pizza sauce thinly and evenly over the dough, leaving about 1/2 inch at the edges for the crust. Layer the pizza with toppings of your choice — crumbled Italian sausage, raw sliced mushrooms, chopped peppers, onions, olives, anchovies, pepperoni — whatever you like!

After you have arranged your toppings, sprinkle the pizza liberally with Parmesan cheese, Asiago cheese, and shredded or sliced mozzarella. Drizzle the pizza with olive oil and bake at 475° for about 20 minutes, or until the crust is golden brown and the cheese is bubbly.

Anna Pastore (below) and Janet Paquin (right) were the master pizza makers at Ecobelli's. At bottom right Adam, Laurina's great-grandson, learns the art from me at home, using a vintage pizza pan from Ecobelli's. ~ Lora Lee

PIZZA MAKER—Anna Pastore, champion pizza maker at the Tam O'Shanter for several years, is coaching Stephen Merola, shown here, in the art of making pizza a la Ecobelli.

Garlic Knots

DOUGH

ACTIVE DRY YEAST	1 (.25 oz) pkg
WATER, warm	1 cup
BREAD FLOUR	2 cups
OLIVE OIL, extra virgin	2 tbsps
SEA SALT, fine	1 tsp

DRESSING

OLIVE OIL, extra virgin	1-1/2 cups
PARMIGIANO CHEESE	1/2 cup
GARLIC, chopped fine	3 cloves
PARSLEY, fresh, chopped fine	1 tbsp
SALT	1 tsp
BLACK PEPPER, fresh ground	1/2 tsp
OREGANO, dried	1 tsp

*PREPARED BY
Lora Lee Ecobelli
Saugerties, NY*

*PHOTO BY
Richard Vang
Knox, NY*

In a small bowl, dissolve yeast in warm water. Let stand until creamy, about 10 minutes.

In a larger bowl, combine the flour, olive oil and salt. Make a well in the center of the flour and pour the yeast in the center. Using a spatula, draw in the ingredients, working from the outside in, and then mix with your hands to form a firm dough that pulls away from the bowl.

Knead the dough briefly on a floured work board just until it takes on more flour and is not sticking to your hands.

Place the dough in a lightly oiled bowl. Score the top on the dough and rub with a little oil to prevent cracking, and cover with a dish towel. Let the dough rise in a warm place until it doubles in size, about 1 to 2 hours.

When the dough has doubled in size, punch it down with your fist to prevent air bubbles. Place it back down on your floured work board. Divide the dough into sections that are easier to work with. Using your hands, pull off small sections of the dough and roll it between your fingers into 6-inch long ropes. Tie the ropes into knots and place them on a greased cookie pan. Bake at 450° for about 10 minutes, or until golden brown. The knots will double in size.

In the meantime, make the dressing by mixing all the ingredients in a large stainless steel bowl or pan. While the knots are still hot from the oven, transfer them to the dressing bowl, and toss them well to evenly coat them with the dressing. Serve immediately.

Nowadays these things are popular, but we like to think our mother, Mary, invented them. She used to coat the bread knots with seasonings by shaking them in a big plastic bag. We couldn't wait to dig into them. Our father loved them so much he started serving them in the restaurant. They are crazy good and it's impossible to eat just one, so save them for special occasions. ~ Lora Lee

A young Mary D'Elisiis Ecobelli in her dance costume.

The Ecobelli "Coat of Arms" Logo

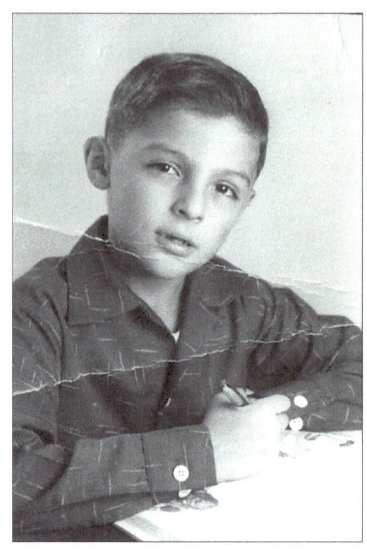

I designed the restaurant logo as part of an art project for school. At the time I lived with my grandmother and ate dinner each night with the staff before the restaurant opened at 5PM. I talked to them about important things to include on the logo. The American flag and the Italian flag were intended to reflect both the family heritage and the pride the family felt in being US citizens. I thought "Ecobelli's" needed to be included because that is what most of the people in the community called the restaurant. It seemed equally important to have "Tam O'Shanter Inn" on it since that was the name our family had retained from the previous owner in an attempt to maintain any following that restaurant had and consequently our family always referred to the restaurant as "The Tam". Those are the things I tried to balance on the logo and then added the 1947 to indicate the year the restaurant was established. ~ Stephen Merola

PASTA SAUCES

A SAUCE OF PRIDE	0.32
"LENA"	0.33
SPAGHETTI SAUCE	0.34
MEATBALLS	0.35
MARINARA SAUCE	0.36
BOLOGNESE SAUCE	0.37
PUTTANESCA SAUCE	0.38
SPAGHETTI CARUSO	0.39

Not only was the Ecobelli logo well-known, but so was the name.

A Sauce of Pride

Italians are fiercely proud of their pasta sauce recipes. Recipes were handed down through the generations but hardly ever written down on paper. Both women and men are highly protective and competitive and sometimes will take their sauce recipes to the grave. We view our sauce as a birthright and an extension of our soul. Dramatic? You bet!

For some of us who grew up in Italian families, the only way to express ourselves was through food. Our memories of family are almost always connected to food, and we frequently reminisce about which aunt made the best pizza dough or which one made the best meatballs. Such musings could cause some relatives to form heated alliances, which in turn could lead to lots of crazy drama. But Italians are known as passionate people and our pride in our cooking is a good metaphor for the ethics we live by.

Everyone tried to make a pasta sauce as good as Laurina, but no one ever came close. She was a master in the kitchen and could make a mouth-watering meal for twenty with any ingredients she happened to have in her pantry. The selection below was featured in the restaurant's menu and shows an example of fierce Italian pride. ~ Lora Lee

---

Italian Cuisine

Contrary to popular belief, Italy is the mother of continental European cuisine. Going back to ancient Romans, Italy's fame in the culinary field came long before that of France. Although French cuisine has taken on its own characteristics, it grew to some degree directly out of the Italian.

Italian dishes are traditional and have been influenced very little by other countries. Many popular foods such as vegetables, salad greens and wines were used in the days of Nero in much the same way as in present day Italy.

The basis of most Italian dishes are tomatoes, garlic and olive oil. Yet, foods in Italy are as diversified as they are traditional. It is not at all unusual to find an Italian who likes neither tomato sauce nor garlic—he probably has his spaghetti with butter and cheese sauce and prefers Melon and Prosciutto to an ordinary antipasto course.

From the Alps to Sicily—these dishes listed in our menu are designed to bring you Italian cuisine at its finest.

THE ECOBELLI FAMILY

A repast without wine is like a day without sunshine

MAY WE SUGGEST:

with antipasto	— Cocktail or Dry Sherry
Seafood or light entree	— Chablis, Dry Sauterne
Spaghetti or macaroni	— Chianti, Burgundy
Steaks, Chops, Fowl	— Chianti, Bardolini
Desserts	— Sauternes
Cheese, Fruits	— Rich Port, Sherry

Harmony between wine and food is of great importance to those who wish to derive the fullest enjoyment from both. However, many diners prefer to partake of only one type of wine throughout the meal. To these, Chianti, Burgundy, Dry Sauternes are recommended.

"Lena"

The following passage is a monologue from Lora Lee Ecobelli's stage-play "Kitchen Tales." In this speech, Lena, an eccentric Italian-American woman, explains why her spaghetti sauce is so important to her.

Never criticize an Italian woman's spaghetti sauce! The wrath of all humanity will come crashing down on your head and you'll never be trusted again. It's the ultimate mortal sin. People just don't understand the importance of what goes into a good sauce. It's not just tomatoes, garlic and olive oil, it's all our hopes and dreams and desires, simmering slowly on the stove. There's almost something erotic about making sauce. The tender way you brown the garlic in the olive oil, filling the house with seductive smells. Onions sautéing till they're just transparent enough, kinda like me. The lusty fragrance of basil and parsley, an aroma so intense it sends shivers through my whole body! And oh, yes, the spices! Each woman has her own distinct blend. I like lots of oregano and red hot pepper flakes; they cloud my head with a sizzling fever. And oh yes, I love the way my hands smell after chopping garlic. A earthy perfume that can linger on my fingertips for days …

You know I feel totally honest and naked when I'm cooking sauce, but I also feel something even more primal than that. I feel the ghosts of all my ancestors whispering their deepest, most intimate secrets in my ears. So don't you dare tell me that my sauce is too spicy, or not sweet enough, or, even worse, not as good as your mother's! You will have opened a wound so deep and wide that you might never taste these delicacies again! Ask any Italian woman you know, and they'll all tell you the same thing.

We guard our legacies with a fierce Mediterranean fire that may seem irrational to some, but to us it's a fight to the death! We have to protect the integrity of all our little Italian grandmothers, whose blood and sweat are the real stock for this sauce! Women who had the magical powers to heal the sick with just a meatball on a fork! Okay, I admit, maybe I'm being a little bit neurotic, but I feel like you're insulting the very nature of my being when you question the validity of my spaghetti sauce. After all, it is my inheritance!

Spaghetti Sauce

INGREDIENTS

OLIVE OIL, extra virgin	1/3 cup
ONION, large, chopped	1
GARLIC, sliced thin	5 cloves
OREGANO, dried	1 tbsp
BASIL, dried or 1 small fresh bunch	1 tbsps
KOSHER SALT, coarse	1 tbsp (to taste)
BLACK PEPPER, fresh ground	1 tbsp
CRUSHED RED PEPPER FLAKES (optional)	to taste
TOMATOES, whole, peeled	1 (28 oz) can
TOMATO PASTE	3 (6 oz) cans
WATER	4 cups
ITALIAN SAUSAGE (optional) and / or MEATBALLS (see recipe on page 35)	1 lb

PREPARED BY Richard Vang Knox, NY

PHOTO BY Richard Vang Knox, NY

In a large sauce pot, sauté the onions and garlic in olive oil on medium heat until tender (do not brown). Add the oregano, basil, salt, black pepper and red pepper flakes (optional) to release their flavors, about 5 minutes.

Empty the can of tomatoes into a bowl, including the juice and crush the tomatoes with a fork. Add the tomatoes (and the juice), tomato paste and water to the pot.

In another frying pan, brown the sausage (and/or meatballs) quickly to sear in the juices. Drain, then transfer to the sauce pot. The meat will continue to cook in the sauce for several hours.

Reduce the heat to low and simmer uncovered. The sauce must cook for at least 4 hours, but it is even better if it is simmered slowly all day — a good sauce takes patience and should never be rushed.

Most Italian sauces begin with onions and garlic sautéed in olive oil until tender. This is to release the core flavors before you add your other ingredients. There are many variations; some recipes call for carrots, some for celery and some for mushrooms for a richer taste, but onions and garlic are the root of most Italian sauces. ~ Lora Lee

Every Sunday after church we'd visit a different relative's house where a huge Italian feast was waiting. Even blindfolded, I would have known who we were visiting by the unique smell of the tomato sauce cooking on the stove. Laurina's smelled savory and rich, Aunt Angie's like garlic and onions, Aunt Anna's tangy and sharp. Seconds and thirds were always on the menu along with a great big bag of leftovers to take home. Wonderful memories! ~ Tom

Meatballs

INGREDIENTS

BEEF, ground chuck or round	2 lbs
PORK, ground (optional)	1/2 lb
EGGS	2
GARLIC, crushed	4 cloves
PARMESAN CHEESE, grated	1/2 cup
BREAD CRUMBS	1 cup
PARSLEY, fresh, chopped	2 tbsps
OREGANO, dried	1 tsp
KOSHER SALT	1 tsp
BLACK PEPPER, fresh ground	1 tsp
OLIVE OIL, extra virgin	1 tbsp

IMAGE FROM Vintage Ecobelli's Restaurant Menu

(makes about 12 meatballs)

Add all the ingredients (except the olive oil) into a large bowl and mix well.

Heat the olive oil to medium-high in a frying pan (cast iron works best). To test the seasoning of the meat mixture, drop a small amount into the hot oil to cook. When done, taste the cooked sample and adjust the seasonings of the raw mixture to taste and mix well.

Roll the meat mixture into balls (meatballs, *capice?*) and brown them in the hot oil to sear in the juices. Leaving the fat in the pan, remove the meatballs and add them to a pot of sauce that is already cooking. You don't need to cook them all the way through because they will continue to cook in the simmering sauce. If you plan to freeze them or use them later, you might want to cook the meatballs more thoroughly and let them drain on a paper towel to remove more of the fat.

To make a good meatball you have to get down and dirty and use your hands. A fattier cut of meat, such as ground chuck or ground round will work best. If you like ground pork, you can also add a half pound of that to the beef mixture. I like mine with just beef, but Laurina used both for a richer flavor.

When I was about fourteen my best friend Susan and I worked in the restaurant coat room. It was an easy job and there was a lot of down time. As long as we did our job, we were free to goof off, which we did enthusiastically. The coat closet was next to the bar where there was always a free buffet of tiny meatballs for the patrons to enjoy while they were waiting for a table or drinking at the bar. Sue and I would fill up salad bowls of meatballs and bring them back to the coat room where we would gorge ourselves silly. And occasionally we would slyly convince the old bartender Babs to give us each a rum and coke to add to our feast. Okay, I confess, we were a couple of renegades, but we sure had a blast. Many times the hostess, Barbara, would come in to reprimand us for our loud giggles but she never ratted us out. Even now, many years later, Sue and I laugh about our outlaw days stealing meatballs in the coat room.
~ Lora Lee

Marinara Sauce

INGREDIENTS

OLIVE OIL, extra virgin	1/4 cup
ANCHOVY PASTE	1 tsp
ONION, chopped	1 cup
GARLIC, sliced fine	6 cloves
PLUM TOMATOES, whole	2 (28 oz) cans
TOMATO PASTE	1 (6 oz) can
PARSLEY, fresh, chopped	1 tsp
OREGANO, dried or fresh	1 tsp
BASIL, dried, crushed (or small fresh bunch)	1 tbsp
KOSHER SALT, coarse	1 tsp or to taste
BLACK PEPPER, fresh ground	1/2 tsp

PREPARED BY
Richard Vang
Knox, NY

PHOTO BY
Richard Vang
Knox, NY

In a large sauce pot, sauté the onions, garlic and anchovy paste in the olive oil over medium-high heat until tender.

Empty the cans of plum tomatoes into a large bowl, including the juice, and break up the tomatoes with a fork. Add the tomatoes and the juice to the pot along with all the remaining ingredients. Simmer until the sauce is thickened and slightly reduced, about 45 minutes. Adjust the seasoning to your taste.

Marinara is a simple red sauce that can be made quickly. It is used as the base for almost all Italian red seafood sauces. When fresh tomatoes are in season, you can substitute them for the canned to make an especially delicious sauce — just blanch, peel, seed and chop. ~ Lora Lee

Dan (lower left) hamming it up with friends and family.

Bolognese Sauce

INGREDIENTS

OLIVE OIL, extra virgin	1/3 cup
ONION, medium, chopped	1
CELERY, chopped fine	2 ribs
CARROT, chopped fine	1
GARLIC, chopped	4 cloves
GARLIC, sliced	4 cloves
BEEF or LAMB, ground	1 lb
ITALIAN SAUSAGE, bulk	1 lb
PORCINI MUSHROOMS, fresh	1/2 lb
BASIL, dried or fresh	1 tsp
OREGANO, dried	1/2 tsp
CRUSHED RED PEPPER FLAKES	to taste
CHIANTI (or another Italian red wine)	1 cup
ITALIAN PLUM TOMATOES, whole	1 (28 oz) can
TOMATO PASTE	3 (6 oz) cans
WATER	3 cups
PARMESAN CHEESE, grated (for garnish)	
BLACK PEPPER, fresh ground (for garnish)	

PREPARED BY
Frank Rebco
Painted Post, NY

PHOTO BY
Frank Rebco
Painted Post, NY

In a large sauce pot, sauté the chopped onion, celery, carrots, mushrooms and garlic in the olive oil. When the vegetables are tender, add the ground beef or lamb, sausage, basil, oregano and red pepper flakes. Brown lightly. Add the wine, whole plum tomatoes, tomato paste and water. Simmer for about 1 hour. Serve over pasta. Sprinkle with grated Parmesan cheese and fresh ground pepper.

This is a quick meat sauce that is hearty yet elegant and a great party dish for a small budget. I used porcini mushrooms in this recipe because I love the flavor, but any variety can be used. I also prefer using ground lamb instead of ground beef because it gives the sauce a richer flavor, reminiscent of the mountainous region of Benevento, Italy, where our grandfather was from. You may serve it over any of the heavier pasta varieties such as rigatoni, but personally I love it on homemade pasta, cut into 1/2-inch strips (see recipe on page 44).

Our grandfather was an avid mushroom hunter. Armed with a battered old colander he and I would hike into the woods in pursuit of the delicacies. When he came upon the desired kind, he would act like a kid who had just struck gold. Then, proudly like he was carrying rare diamonds, he would bring them home to Laurina so she could turn them into his favorite dishes.

But Grandpa's mushroom-hunting days came to an abrupt halt when he became ill after eating a poisonous variety. His way of determining if a mushroom was edible was to put the mushroom in a pot of boiling water, then drop a silver dollar into the water. If the silver turned black, the mushroom was supposedly poisonous. If not, it was okay. In retrospect it was a bit like Russian roulette because wild mushrooms can look alike and varieties can easily be mistaken. Even though our grandfather had been gathering mushrooms his whole life, this one mistake almost cost him that life — so be careful if you go mushroom hunting. Do your research and take along a knowledgeable person. ~ Lora Lee

Puttanesca Sauce

INGREDIENTS

OLIVE OIL	1/4 cup
ONION, chopped fine	1 cup
GARLIC, sliced fine	6 cloves
PLUM TOMATOES, whole	2 (28 oz) cans
KALAMATA OLIVES, pitted, halved	1 cup
TOMATO PASTE	2 tbsps
PARSLEY, fresh, chopped	1 tbsp
OREGANO, dried	1/2 tsp
CAPERS, drained	2 tbsps
ANCHOVY FILLETS, minced (~4 fillets)	1 tbsp
BASIL, dried, crushed	1/2 tsp
or small fresh bunch	1
CRUSHED RED PEPPER FLAKES	1/2 tsp
SALT, coarse	to taste
BLACK PEPPER, fresh ground	to taste
ROMANO CHEESE, for garnish	

PREPARED BY
Lora Lee Ecobelli
Saugerties, NY

PHOTO BY
Lora Lee Ecobelli
Saugerties, NY

In a large sauce pot, sauté the onions and garlic in the olive oil over medium-high heat until tender. Do not brown.

Empty the cans of plum tomatoes into a large bowl, including the juice. Break the tomatoes into pieces with a fork. Add the tomatoes (and the juice) and the remaining ingredients. Simmer until the sauce is thickened and slightly reduced, about 45 minutes.

Before serving, adjust the seasoning to taste. Serve over pasta, cooked *al dente*, and sprinkle with grated Romano cheese.

Ah yes, the pasta of the whores! This is a delicious sauce that is also great served over your favorite broiled fish. Or, even better, poach the fish in the sauce. For some reason, this was our grandfather's all-time favorite, but I'm not going to read too much into that! ~ Lora Lee

Truth be told, our grandfather was probably more of a mascot than a hard worker at the restaurant. Our father and Laurina did most of the daily back-breaking stuff while Grandpa would hang out at the bar, tell stories and play his mandolin. He was also fond of taking little "trips" — disappearing for a while, maybe to Italy, Cuba or his favorite, Spain. Did his adventures gallivanting around the world contribute to his love of Puttanesca sauce? Maybe, but like Lora Lee, I'm not going to read too much into that either! ~ Tom

Dan enjoying a few beers, sometime in the 1930's.

Spaghetti Caruso

INGREDIENTS

BUTTER	4 tbsps
ONION, medium, sliced	1
CHICKEN LIVERS, chopped in large pieces	2 pints
GARLIC, chopped	2 cloves
SEASONED FLOUR (salt, pepper, garlic powder)	1/2 cup
RED WINE, dry	1/2 cup
SALT	1 tsp
BLACK PEPPER, fresh ground	1/2 tsp
MARINARA SAUCE (see recipe on page 36)	2 cups

In a sauté pan, melt the butter and add the onions and garlic, sautéing until tender. Meanwhile, in a bowl make the seasoned flour by mixing a pinch of salt, pepper and garlic powder with a 1/2 cup of flour. Dredge the chicken livers in seasoned flour and add them to the pan, browning quickly, about 5 minutes. Add the wine and scrape up all the bits of the cooked ingredients. Add the marinara sauce and let simmer for about 10 more minutes, until the chicken liver is no longer pink but not overcooked. Serve over spaghetti.

*PREPARED BY
Lora Lee Ecobelli
Saugerties, NY*

*PHOTO BY
Lora Lee Ecobelli
Saugerties, NY*

Italians love organ meat but I will spare you some of the weird things that I grew up with and offer you instead this delicious recipe for chicken livers that was featured in the restaurant. ~ Lora Lee

Mary Ecobelli (center) with colleagues at a General Electric lunch room in the 1940's.

Ecobelli's Waitresses & Staff

The people who worked for our grandparents and our father were not just employees — they were like family — and, in fact, some were family. It would be impossible to name all of them; some worked at Ecobelli's for decades, and some for just a summer. These photos bring back fond memories, and I hope they do for you too. ~ Lora Lee

 Ecobelli's Restaurant, in Ballston Spa, has always been proud to serve you the finest in Italian and American cuisine...and now... Ralph Ecobelli is proud to introduce you to the people who have made his restaurant so popular! People like Anita Strobeck of Ballston Spa. Anita has been part of the Ecobelli family since 1952. Originally from Sweden, her hobbies include knitting and sewing. Anita's favorite dish is Veal Scalopino Lemon, a special this week for only $5.00. Why not come in this week and say "Hello" to Anita. She will be happy to serve you her favorite dish!

Ecobelli's Tam O'Shanter
Route 50, Ballston Spa. Open Tues-Sat.

Be sure to listen each week for the Ecobelli's staff salute on

JANE, ESTHER, BARBARA, JUNE, ANITA, JOE, LAURA, TERRY, RALPH, MATT, GEORGE, MIKE, RAY.

Amy Ryder (right, with Dan) was the bookkeeper for the restaurant for many years. She was outgoing and fun, with a twangy Texas accent. As a six- or seven-year-old kid, I just loved her. I would bring her love letters and draw her pictures. She lived close to the restaurant and I'd help her and her husband rake their lawn, dust the house — anything to spend time with her. Her husband was an artist and coin collector and I would spend hours with him too. They were wonderful people. ~ Tom

36th ANNIVERSARY
COCKTAIL PARTY FOR

ANITA

Ecobelli's 7:30 PM
Monday, Jan. 30, 1989
Donation $7.50

GOURMET RINGSIDE

Ecobelli's Restaurant in Ballston Spa has always been proud to serve you the finest in Italian and American cuisine...and now...Ralph Ecobelli is proud to introduce you to the people who have made his restaurant so popular!...People like Raymond Maxfield of Malta. Raymond has been part of the Ecobelli family since 1959. His hobbies are fishing and snowmobiling, and his favorite dish is Spaghetti and Meatballs, a special this week for $.50 off the original price. Why not come in this week and say "hello" to Raymond. He will be happy to have you try his favorite dish. Ecobelli's Restaurant, Route 50, Ballston Spa: Open Tuesday through Sunday.

Closed Thanksgiving Day.

Now Open Sundays 1-9 p.m.

Ecobelli's Tam O'Shanter
Route 50, Ballston Spa
open Tues - Sun
Be sure to listen each week for the Ecobelli's staff salute on **WROW** 59 AM FM-STEREO 95

GOURMET RINGSIDE

Ecobelli's Restaurant in Ballston Spa has always been proud to serve you the finest in Italian and American cuisine...and now...Ralph Ecobelli is proud to introduce you to the people who have made his restaurant so popular...people like Bill Martone of Saratoga Springs, our cook since last September. His hobby is golf and his favorite dish is Veal Marsala, a special this week for only $1.00 off the regular price. Why not come in this week and say "hello" to Bill. He will be happy to have you try his favorite dish. Ecobelli's Restaurant, Route 50, Ballston Spa: Open Tuesday through Sunday.

Now Open Sundays 1-9 p.m.

Ecobelli's Tam O'Shanter
Route 50, Ballston Spa
open Tues - Sun
Be sure to listen each week for the Ecobelli's staff salute on **WROW** 59 AM FM-STEREO 95

GOURMET RINGSIDE

Ecobelli's Restaurant in Ballston Spa has always been proud to serve you the finest in Italian and American cuisine...and now...Ralph Ecobelli is proud to introduce you to the people who have made his restaurant so popular!...People like Anna Pastore of Ballston Spa. Anna has been part of the Ecobelli family since 1955. Her hobbies are cooking and sewing, and her favorite dish is veal braggiola — a special this week for $1.00 off our regular price! Why not come in this week and say "hello" to Anna. She will be happy to have you try her favorite dish. Ecobelli's Restaurant, Route 50, Ballston Spa: Open Tuesday through Saturday.

Now Open Sundays 1-9 p.m.

Ecobelli's Tam O'Shanter
Route 50, Ballston Spa
open Tues - Sun
Be sure to listen each week for the Ecobelli's staff salute on **WROW** 59 AM FM-STEREO 95

PASTA DISHES

FRESH EGG PASTA & RAVIOLI DOUGH	0.44
WATER GLASS RAVIOLI	0.45
LAURINA'S FAMOUS LASAGNA	0.46
EGGPLANT PARMIGIANA	0.47
ZITI SICILIAN	0.48

Fresh Egg Pasta & Ravioli Dough

EGG PASTA INGREDIENTS

FLOUR, all-purpose, unbleached or SEMOLINA FLOUR	2 cups
SALT	1/2 tsp
EGGS, large	3

(Makes 1 lb pasta.)

Sift the salt and the flour together. On a clean work board, make a mound out of the flour mixture, then make a deep well in the center. (You can use a large mixing bowl if that helps.) Break the eggs into the well. Whisk the eggs with a fork, gradually incorporating the flour from the sides of the well. When the dough mixture becomes too thick to mix with the fork, begin kneading it with your hands.

PREPARED BY Adira Amram & Bram Muller New York, NY

PHOTO BY Bram Muller New York, NY

Knead the dough for about 10 minutes, until it is smooth and supple. Dust the dough and the work surface with more flour as needed to keep the dough from sticking to your hands. When it is at the right consistency, shape it into a ball. Wrap the dough tightly in plastic wrap and allow it to rest at room temperature for 30 minutes.

Roll out the dough with a pasta machine or a floured rolling pin to the thickness of the pasta type you want to make. Use a pasta machine or a sharp knife to cut the pasta into your desired shape, then powder the pasta with flour and let it dry.

To cook your pasta, bring salted water to a boil in a large pot. Cook the pasta until it is *al dente*. Drain the pasta well and dress it with your favorite sauce.

RAVIOLI DOUGH INGREDIENTS

FLOUR, all-purpose, unbleached or SEMOLINA FLOUR	3-1/2 cups
SALT	1 tsp
EGGS, large	6
OLIVE OIL, extra virgin	1 tsp

Follow the instructions as above, except add the olive oil to the well along with the eggs. Follow the instructions above again until you put the dough to rest. Then follow instructions for Water Glass Ravioli (page 45) or Bramram's Ravioli (page 74).

Laurina made fresh pasta for the family whenever there was a special occasion. There is nothing like the flavor and texture of freshly made pasta. It melts in your mouth. Laurina never used a pasta machine, although it does make life easier. She cut the pasta into strips and laid them across broom handles in the kitchen to dry. She used this recipe to make her amazing water glass ravioli which, believe me, were to die for. ~ Lora Lee

Water Glass Ravioli

RAVIOLI DOUGH

See the recipe for Ravioli Dough on page 44.

CHEESE FILLING

RICOTTA CHEESE	2 cups
MOZZARELLA CHEESE, shredded	1/2 cup
PARMESAN CHEESE, grated	1/2 cup
or ROMANO, ASIAGO or PROVOLONE CHEESE	
SALT	1/2 tsp (to taste)
BLACK PEPPER, fresh ground	1/2 tsp
PARSLEY, fresh, chopped fine	2 tsps
EGG, beaten	1

PREPARED BY Richard Vang Knox, NY

PHOTO BY Richard Vang Knox, NY

While your ravioli dough is resting, prepare your filling.

In a large mixing bowl, mix together all the cheeses, salt and pepper. Taste test the mixture for seasoning and add more as needed. (Always start with less salt and pepper — you can't take it out, but you can always add more!) Add the chopped parsley and the beaten egg and mix well.

With a floured rolling pin or a pasta machine, roll out two thin (less than 1/8 inch), long sheets of pasta. With a rolling pin you can make bigger sheets (about 12-inch squares) than with a machine, but it is harder work by hand. Use more flour if needed to keep the sheets from sticking.

Drop about 1 tablespoon of the filling mixture onto the dough, and continue in a grid pattern about 3 inches apart. Brush a little water around each dollop of filling.

Cover the pasta sheet and filling with the other sheet of pasta, pressing firmly around the filling to make an air-tight seal. Using an overturned water or juice glass as a cutter, cut out the individual ravioli and remove them from the sheets. Pinch down the edges of each with a fork to secure the seal. Sprinkle each lightly with flour to dry.

To cook your ravioli, bring salted water to a boil in a large pot. Cook the ravioli for just a few minutes; they will float to the surface when they are done. Drain well and dress the ravioli simply with melted butter or with your favorite sauce.

Laurina's Famous Lasagna

INGREDIENTS

SWEET ITALIAN SAUSAGE, bulk	1 lb
GROUND BEEF, lean	1 lb
MUSHROOMS, sliced	1 lb
SPAGHETTI SAUCE (see recipe on page 34)	8 cups
LASAGNA NOODLES	1 lb
RICOTTA CHEESE, fresh	48 oz (3 lbs)
MOZZARELLA CHEESE, shredded	1 lb
PARMESAN CHEESE, grated	1 cup
EGGS	6
PARSLEY, fresh, chopped	4 tbsps

PREPARED BY
Lora Lee Ecobelli
Saugerties, NY

PHOTO BY
Lora Lee Ecobelli
Saugerties, NY

In a heavy Dutch oven over medium heat, cook the sausage, ground beef and mushrooms until browned. Drain off the excess grease and stir in 4 cups of the spaghetti sauce. Simmer, uncovered, for about 30 minutes. The sauce should reduce and thicken slightly. Remove the Dutch oven from the heat and set aside.

Bring a large pot of salted water to a boil. Cook the lasagna noodles in boiling water until *al dente*. Drain the noodles, rinse them well with cold water, and spread each noodle out flat on a large oiled plate to prevent them from sticking together. (You could also skip this step by substituting oven-ready lasagna noodles.)

Preheat the oven to 375° degrees. In a large mixing bowl, combine the ricotta cheese, half of the mozzarella cheese, half of the Parmesan cheese, the eggs and the parsley. When mixed well, slowly fold in the cooled meat-mushroom-sauce mixture.

To assemble the lasagna, spread 1-1/2 cups of the remaining meat-mushroom-sauce mixture in the bottom of a deep-dish 12 x 16-inch lasagna or baking pan. Arrange about 6 noodles lengthwise over meat sauce to cover the bottom of the pan. Spread with one half of the ricotta cheese-meat-sauce mixture. Repeat with a second layer, and top with the remaining halves of the mozzarella and Parmesan cheeses. Cover with foil. (To prevent the cheese from sticking to the foil, spray the foil with cooking spray before covering the pan.)

Bake for 35 minutes. Remove the foil, and bake for an additional 25 minutes. Let the lasagna cool for 15 minutes before serving. To serve, cut the lasagna into squares and top each serving with remaining spaghetti sauce.

GOURMET RINGSIDE

Ecobelli's Restaurant in Ballston Spa has always been proud to serve you the finest in Italian and American cuisine...and now...Ralph Ecobelli is proud to introduce you to the people who have made his restaurant so popular!...People like Joan Voelker of Ballston Spa. Joan has been part of the Ecobelli family for three months. Her hobby is bowling, and her favorite dish is Lasagna — special this week for only 50 cents off regular price. Why not come in this week and say "hello" to Joan. She will be happy to have you try her favorite dish! Ecobelli's Restaurant, Route 50, Ballston Spa. Open Tuesday through Sunday.

Now Open Sundays 1-9 p.m.
Route 50, Ballston Spa
open Tues - Sun

Be sure to listen each week for the Ecobelli's staff salute on

This was the restaurant's biggest selling entree. People from everywhere get nostalgic when they talk about this mouth-watering deep-dish lasagna. It was our grandmother's signature dish and her proudest creation. I can still see her standing in the corner of the dining room with a big smile on her face, watching her customers enjoy their meal.
~ Lora Lee

Eggplant Parmigiana

INGREDIENTS

EGGPLANT, peeled, sliced in thin rounds	2 large
SEASONED FLOUR	1 cup
(salt, black pepper, garlic powder, dried parsley)	
BREAD CRUMBS	1 cup
EGGS	5
OLIVE OIL, light, or VEGETABLE OIL	1/2 cup
SPAGHETTI or MARINARA SAUCE	2 cups
PARMESAN CHEESE, grated	1/2 cup
MOZZARELLA CHEESE, shredded	1-1/2 cups

PREPARED BY Lora Lee Ecobelli Saugerties, NY

PHOTO BY Lora Lee Ecobelli Saugerties, NY

Peel and slice the eggplant thinly, and sprinkle the slices with salt to stop discoloration and release the excess water. (This will also remove any bitterness.) In a bowl, make the seasoned flour by mixing a pinch each of salt, pepper, garlic powder and dried parsley with the flour and the bread crumbs. Whisk the eggs in another bowl.

Heat the oil to medium-high. Dip the eggplant slices in the flour mixture, then the egg, then the flour mixture again to create a nice crust. Fry the slices in the oil until golden brown, and set them aside on a plate lined with paper towels to drain the excess oil. Preheat the oven to 350°.

Pour some of the spaghetti sauce (page 34) or marinara sauce (page 36) into the bottom of a ceramic baking pan, and spread evenly. Line the pan with your first layer of fried eggplant slices. Sprinkle the slices with more sauce, then some Parmesan and mozzarella cheese. Repeat this process to build as many layers as you like. Top the last layer with the remaining sauce and cheese. Bake at 350° for about 45 minutes, or until the cheese is brown and bubbly.

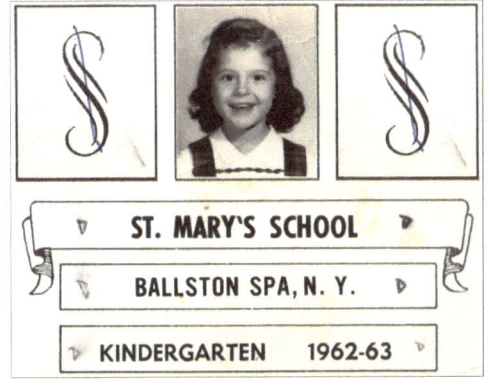

ST. MARY'S SCHOOL — BALLSTON SPA, N.Y. — KINDERGARTEN 1962-63

When I was a kid Laurina used to make for my lunch box these huge sandwiches of eggplant parmigiana on thick slices of Italian bread. Back then I didn't celebrate the uniqueness of my restaurant family like I do now, and I was embarrassed by these over-the-top sandwiches. All I wanted was to be like all the other kids with their wimpy little sandwiches of peanut butter and jelly on mushy white bread. So I would trade my eggplant for their gummy mess, thinking that I was the one who made out good. Several years ago I heard from an old school buddy who remembered my embarrassed trading. "We sure made out like bandits," he said. "We thought you were a real sucker. We used to fight over who got to trade with you!" ~ Lora Lee

My best friend Mike (right) in the 9th grade after he scored one of my school lunches containing an eggplant sandwich and a ritzy side of wine cheese and crackers. ~ Tom

Ziti Sicilian

INGREDIENTS

EGGPLANT, peeled, sliced thin	1 large
SEASONED BREAD CRUMBS	1-1/2 cups
(salt, black pepper, garlic powder, dried parsley)	
FLOUR	1/2 cup
OLIVE OIL, light (or VEGETABLE OIL)	1/2 cup
EGGS	3
ZITI or PENNE pasta	1 lb
RICOTTA CHEESE	16 oz
MOZZARELLA CHEESE, shredded	1-1/2 cups
PARMESAN CHEESE, grated	1/2 cup
BOLOGNESE SAUCE (see recipe on page 37)	6 cups

PREPARED BY
Tom Ecobelli
Los Angeles, CA

PHOTO BY
Tom Ecobelli
Los Angeles, CA

Peel and slice the eggplant thinly, and sprinkle the slices with salt to stop discoloration and release the excess water. In a bowl, make the seasoned bread crumbs by mixing a pinch of salt, pepper, garlic powder and dried parsley with 1-1/2 cups of bread crumbs and the flour. Whisk the eggs in another bowl.

Heat the oil to medium-high. Dip the eggplant slices in the bread crumb mixture, then the egg, then the bread crumb mixture again to create a nice crust. Fry the slices in the oil until golden brown, and set them aside on a plate lined with paper towels to drain the excess oil.

To cook your ziti, bring salted water to a boil in a large pot, and cook to *al dente*. Drain the ziti well and pour it into a large bowl. Mix in the three cheeses (reserving 1/2 cup of the mozzarella for the topping) and 3 cups of the Bolognese sauce. Mix well and pour the mixture into a large, oiled lasagna pan.

Layer the fried eggplant slices on top of the ziti mixture. Top the eggplant with the remaining 3 cups of sauce, the reserved 1/2 cup of mozzarella, and a liberal sprinkling of extra Parmesan cheese. Cover with aluminum foil and bake for 20 minutes at 350°, then uncover and bake for an additional 15 minutes, until the surface is brown and bubbly.

To serve, cut the ziti into large squares (like lasagna) and top each serving with more sauce. Like most pasta casseroles, this gets even better the next day, so be prepared to send home some leftovers with your dinner guests.

GOURMET RINGSIDE

Ecobelli's Restaurant in Ballston Spa has always been proud to serve you the finest in Italian and American cuisine...and now...Ralph Ecobelli is proud to introduce you to the people who have made his restaurant so popular!...People like Frieda Voehringer of Ballston Spa. Frieda has been part of the Ecobelli family for one year. Her hobby is training and showing Hackney and Shetland Ponies, and her favorite dish is Ziti Sicilian — a special this week for 50 cents off regular price. Why not come in this week and say "hello" to Frieda. She will be happy to have you try her favorite dish! Ecobelli's Restaurant, Route 50, Ballston Spa: Open Tuesday through Sunday.

Now Open Sundays 1-9 p.m.

Ecobelli's Tam O'Shanter
Be sure to listen each week for the Ecobelli's staff salute on

Closed Christmas Day and New Year's Day
Route 50, Ballston Spa
open Tues - Sun

WROW 59 AM · FM STEREO 95

This is Laurina's version of the classic baked pasta. I like it better than lasagna. It's a rich, inexpensive party dish when you need to cook for a crowd.
~ Lora Lee

I can still hear Laurina, my mother, or any number of my aunts plopping gobs of Ziti Sicilian onto my plate, saying, "Eat, eat! Don't be ashamed!" Even though the recipe was basically the same, it was always delicious and unique to the person who made it.
~ Tom

SEAFOOD

MUSSELS MARINARA	0.50
SHRIMP FRA DIAVOLO	0.51
ZUPPA DE PESCA	0.52
SHRIMP WITH PEAS AND PIMIENTOS	0.54
LINGUINE WITH WHITE CLAM SAUCE	0.55

When she was younger, Laurina worked for her uncle's seafood company.

Mussels Marinara

INGREDIENTS

MUSSELS, scrubbed, beards removed	2 dozen
OLIVE OIL, extra virgin	1/4 cup
GARLIC, chopped	4 cloves
WHITE WINE, dry	1 cup
KOSHER SALT	1 tsp
BLACK PEPPER, fresh ground	1/2 tsp
BAY LEAF	1
MARINARA SAUCE (see recipe on page 36)	2 cups
CRUSHED RED PEPPER FLAKES	to taste
ITALIAN PARSLEY, fresh, chopped	2 tbsps

PREPARED BY
Tom Ecobelli
Los Angeles, CA

PHOTO BY
Tom Ecobelli
Los Angeles, CA

Scrub the mussels and remove the beards.

In a large stock pot, heat the olive oil over medium heat. Add the garlic and sauté quickly (do not brown). Add the wine, salt, pepper, bay leaf and red pepper flakes and cook for 1 minute. Add the marinara sauce and then the mussels, stirring to coat them all evenly.

Cover the pot and let steam on medium heat about 8 minutes, or until the mussels open. Discard any unopened mussels. Taste the sauce and adjust the seasonings as needed. Transfer the mussels to a platter, sprinkle each with the chopped parsley, and cover them with the sauce. Serve this dish with a hearty Italian bread for sopping up the sauce.

It took a while after our mom passed away for our father to again find someone special, but once he found Kathy they stayed together for over twenty happy years. I snapped these pictures while they were walking into their favorite seafood restaurant where they would always share an order of Mussels Marinara. I can still hear them laughing and poking each other under the table playing footsies. They were like two bickering, lovable kids, and I'm very happy they found each other. ~ Tom

Shrimp Fra Diavolo

INGREDIENTS

SHRIMP, large, peeled, deveined	1 lb
LINGUINI or other pasta	
CRUSHED RED PEPPER FLAKES	1 tsp
GARLIC, chopped fine	2 cloves
OLIVE OIL	3 tbsps
ONION, small, sliced	1
RED BELL PEPPER, chopped	1/2 cup
WHITE WINE, dry	1/2 cup
MARINARA SAUCE (see recipe on page 36)	2 cups
PARSLEY, fresh, chopped	~ 1/4 bunch
SALT	1/2 tsp (to taste)

PREPARED BY
Richard Vang
Knox, NY

PHOTO BY
Richard Vang
Knox, NY

Prepare the shrimp and toss them in a medium bowl with the red pepper flakes and garlic and set aside. Prepare your pasta now; this dish only takes a few minutes to prepare. Heat the oil in a heavy skillet to medium-high and sauté the onion and red bell pepper until tender. Add the shrimp and sauté for about a minute. Add the white wine and continue cooking until the shrimp just turns pink, about 1 to 2 minutes. Add the marinara sauce and cook for about 5 minutes more. Do not overcook the shrimp. Stir in the parsley and serve over linguine or your favorite pasta.

This is our father's recipe. It was a staple in the restaurant.
~ Lora Lee

As a little kid I used to sneak through the restaurant, stealing morsels of food like a pint-sized kleptomaniac. Laurina and my Dad would have gladly given me whatever I asked for, but where was the excitement in that? When nobody was looking, the first thing I'd snatch was an ice-cold, cooked shrimp from the walk-in cooler and chase it down with a baked meatball. Yep, I had gourmet tastes, even then.
~ Tom

Tom before he went bad and began his shrimp-napping career.

Zuppa de Pesca

INGREDIENTS

OLIVE OIL, extra virgin	1/3 cup
GARLIC, chopped coarse	4 cloves
WHITE WINE, dry	1 cup
CRUSHED RED PEPPER FLAKES (optional)	to taste
WATER	1 cup
SALT	1 tsp
CLAMS, Cherry stone or Littleneck, scrubbed	1 dozen
MUSSELS, scrubbed, beards removed	1 dozen
MARINARA SAUCE (see recipe on page 36)	6 cups
CRAB MEAT, lump	1/2 lb
(or any firm-fleshed fish, cut into 2-inch chunks)	
BAY SCALLOPS	1/2 lb
LOBSTER TAILS, split (optional)	2
SHRIMP, medium, peeled and deveined	1/2 lb
CALAMARI, cleaned, cut into rings	1/2 lb
PARSLEY, chopped coarse	1/4 cup

PREPARED BY
Tom Ecobelli
Los Angeles, CA

PHOTO BY
Tom Ecobelli
Los Angeles, CA

It is probably best to prepare all the ingredients, especially the seafood, before you begin cooking.

Heat the olive oil in a large stainless steel stock pot. Add the garlic, sautéing quickly, then add the wine, red pepper flakes, water and salt. When the liquid begins to boil, add the clams and mussels. Cover the pot until they just steam open. Remove the shellfish from the pot, strain the liquid and reserve to be used later.

In another large stock pot, heat the marinara sauce and cook to reduce slightly. Add the crab meat (or other firm-fleshed fish) and cook for 5 minutes. Add the lobster, shrimp, scallops and calamari, and cook for another few minutes until the lobster is done. (Look for it to be bright red; it doesn't take long.) Slowly add the clams, mussels and all of the reserved broth.

Cover the pot and reduce the heat to low and simmer. The soup will be thinner because of the clam/mussel broth. Taste and adjust salt and pepper to taste. Serve the soup in large bowls, with a crusty garlic bread.

This fish stew is almost like a French bouillabaisse. It was always served on Christmas Eve after midnight mass. The idea is to have a different fish for every day of the week ("Seven Fishes for Christmas"), and in this case, all in one pot. Laurina would change the recipe according to whatever fish was available. She was famous for her special holiday fish dinners at the restaurant.

One of my first memories of our grandmother Laurina has to do with tiny, black periwinkle snails. I couldn't have been more than three years old. I remember walking into the kitchen all dressed up in my red and white Christmas pajamas, looking up and seeing her towering over me at the stove, opening the lid of a huge pot of boiling water. She lifted me up and put me on the counter so I could see what she was doing. She reached down into a brown paper bag and took out a fistful of black snails. I was fascinated. She laughed when she saw my eyes open wide, then she opened the lid of the pot and threw the snails in. As soon as they hit the water they decided it was not the place to be. They proceeded to crawl up and down the sides of the pot, across the counter and onto the floor. I never knew that snails could move that fast. Laurina was laughing as she scooped them up and threw them back into the giant pot of doom. Later on that night she tried to get me to taste one because they were considered a great delicacy. Our grandfather loved them so much he even had a little gold toothpick he kept in his wallet for extracting them but there was no way was I going to put one of those things in my three-year-old mouth. I was still thinking about those poor murdered snails! ~ Lora Lee

"Tramp" the Wonder Dog

Tramp was an old mutt who showed up at the restaurant one day looking for a handout. He was pure white with one black ear and looked just like the dog in the "Our Gang" comedies. He was a vagabond spirit and would disappear for weeks at a time (hence the name "Tramp") but would always come back when he was tired of the road. My dad fed him meatballs and leftover steak bones so he lived high-on-the-hog when he was visiting. He was a really smart dog and learned quite a few tricks from all the adoring customers and employees. He was so lovable that he had total access to the busy kitchen and would lie down next to my father while he was cooking, ready to catch any scraps that might hit the floor.

Tramp really took a shine to me and was extremely protective of his five-year-old ward. He even saved my life one day. It was a particularly snowy winter and the plow trucks had cleared the parking lot and piled a huge mountain of snow up next to the garage. Dressed up like an Eskimo, I went out to play in the snow early in the morning. I was a very independent five-year-old and was always going on solo adventures so my mother wasn't overly concerned, but when dinner time arrived and I had not returned, my panicked family organized a search team. The police were called and everyone scoured the neighborhood, but I was nowhere to be found. Tramp, however, kept running to the top of the snow bank and barking frantically for hours, but no one paid any attention.

Finally, as the stars were beginning to come out, my father climbed the 20-foot mound to get him down and there he found me. I had climbed up the mountain looking for a good place to put my sled but the snow was unstable and I had fallen deep into the bottom of the bank. No one had thought to look up there, but Tramp never left me. Because the snow served as insulation it kept me from freezing to death, but it also muffled my voice, so no one but Tramp could hear my calls for help. He had saved my life. That old pooch was pampered like there was no tomorrow after that, being touted a hero greater than Lassie. ~ Lora Lee

Shrimp with Peas and Pimientos

INGREDIENTS

SHRIMP, medium, peeled, deveined	1 lb
BUTTER	1/2 stick
GARLIC, chopped fine	3 cloves
SALT, coarse	to taste
BLACK PEPPER, fresh ground	to taste
THYME, dried	1/2 tsp
WHITE WINE, dry	1/2 cup
SPANISH PIMENTOS, chopped	1 (3 oz) jar
PEAS, fresh or frozen	1/2 cup
PARSLEY, fresh, chopped	1 tbsp
BASMATI RICE	

PREPARED BY
Laure-Jeanne Davignon
Knox, NY

PHOTO BY
Richard Vang
Knox, NY

Begin the rice a little ahead of time; this dish only takes a few minutes to prepare. Peel and devein the shrimp.

Melt the butter in a heavy pan on medium heat. Add shrimp, garlic, salt, pepper and thyme. Cook for about one minute. Add the wine, pimentos and peas. Toss in the fresh parsley and cook for about 5 minutes, until the shrimp turns pink and the alcohol burns off. Adjust the seasonings to taste. To serve, pour over hot, buttered basmati rice.

This is our mother Mary's recipe. She was an excellent cook in her own right. It looks fancy but it's quick to prepare and makes a festive and delicious party dish.
~ Lora Lee

Linguine with White Clam Sauce

INGREDIENTS

CLAMS, Cherrystone or Littleneck, scrubbed	2 dozen
LINGUINE, dry	1 lb
OLIVE OIL, extra virgin	1/4 cup
GARLIC, chopped coarse	3 cloves
WHITE WINE, dry	1 cup
KOSHER SALT	1/2 tsp (to taste)
CRUSHED RED PEPPER FLAKES (optional)	1/2 tsp
OREGANO, dried	1/2 tsp
BLACK PEPPER, fresh ground	1/2 tsp
ITALIAN PARSLEY, fresh, chopped	3 tbsps

PREPARED BY Elizabeth Breslin Somers, NY

PHOTO BY Elizabeth Breslin Somers, NY

Scrub the clams. Begin the linguine now; this dish only takes a few minutes to prepare.

In a large sauté pan, heat the olive oil over medium heat. Add the garlic and clams and toss them to coat. Add the wine, salt, red pepper flakes, oregano and black pepper. Cover the pan and cook until all the clams are opened, about 5 minutes. Discard any unopened clams. When the linguine is cooked to *al dente*, drain well and mix in the pan with the clam sauce. Add the chopped parsley and toss to combine. Adjust the salt and pepper to taste. Serve with a crusty Italian bread for sopping up the sauce.

This is my variation on our dad's recipe. It takes no time to prepare and is a real knock out, but the real question remains: **To cheese or not to cheese?**

The question of whether or not to sprinkle cheese on fish pasta dishes is hotly debated among Italians, probably for centuries. Our father was of the cheese alliance. I will never forget the fiery argument he had on the night before my wedding with a waiter who refused to give him the Parmesan cheese he requested for his main entree. We were having a very nice dinner in a famous restaurant in New York City's Little Italy. Dad ordered linguini with white clam sauce. Laurina eyed it critically when it came, declaring it didn't look so hot, but maybe cheese would help. He called the waiter over and asked for some. Indignantly, the waiter told him real Italians know better than to order cheese with their clam sauce and refused to give it to him. My father fired back that he was 100% Italian, and that if he wanted cheese on his clam sauce, he would damn well have cheese on it!

Laurina tried to calm our dad down because it was the same restaurant where the famous mobster Joey Gallo was shot and she feared the worst. Finally, the intimidating owner came out, followed by two burly-looking guys. Our father wouldn't back down and argued him into admitting that one of the cardinal rules of good business is that the customer is always right. The owner put up a fight, but when it was all over, the two men were laughing and we were sharing a bottle of wine on the house. And of course, our dad got cheese on his clam sauce. ~ Lora Lee

"Babs" and the Ecobelli's Bar

GOURMET RINGSIDE

Ecobelli's Restaurant in Ballston Spa has always been proud to serve you the finest in Italian and American cuisine...and now...Ralph Ecobelli is proud to introduce you to the people who have made his restaurant so popular!...People like Dominick (Babs) Schiavo of Ballston Spa. "Babs" has been part of the Ecobelli family since 1955. He is a native of Ballston Spa and his hobbies are gardening and remodeling. His favorite drinks are The BOMB and GILHOOEY — specials this week for only $.65!! Why not come in this week and say "hello" to Babs. He will be happy to serve you his favorite drinks. Ecobelli's Restaurant, Route 50, Ballston Spa: Open Tuesday through Saturday.

Ecobelli's Tam O'Shanter
Route 50, Ballston Spa
Open Tues-Sat.
Be sure to listen each week for the Ecobelli's staff salute on WROW 59 AM FM-STEREO 95

Dominick "Babs" Schiavo was the bartender in the restaurant's bar for decades, and many customers were as loyal to him as they were to the food. It was in the bar area that Laurina first started serving food.

In the old news clipping below, the writer claimed that Dan ran a tight ship in the bar. But, as is quite evident in some of the photos, things could get a little out of hand!

DAN AND LAURA ECOBELLI

When Dan and Laura purchased the Tam in 1947, it was a dream fulfilled. Little did they dream from their humble beginning nor did they realize that they would build a reputation in the restaurant business that is now known from coast to coast. When they first started they worked together in building their reputation. Dan would take care of the bar and also play the mandolin to entertain the customers. Laura would be in the kitchen making pizza and popcorn to give to whatever customers were in at the time. As business grew Laura would mingle with the patrons greeting them with a warm smile and make sure their evening at the Tam was enjoyable. Dan was known for his sternness, for he would not allow his employees or his customers to get out of hand. Now after 29 years, Dan has passed away but Laura still has a hand in the operation. We salute Dan and Laura this week by offering a glass of champagne to all customers coming in this week for dinner.

MEAT DISHES

BRACIOLE	0.58
ITALIAN OVEN FRIED CHICKEN	0.59
MADEIRA	0.60
CHICKEN CACCIATORE	0.61
PICATA	0.62
SCALLOPINO	0.63
CHICKEN ROMANO	0.64
BREADED CUTLETS & PARMIGIANA	0.65
ROSEMARY CHICKEN	0.66
EASTER LAMB	0.67
ROAST CHICKEN AND SAUSAGE	0.68

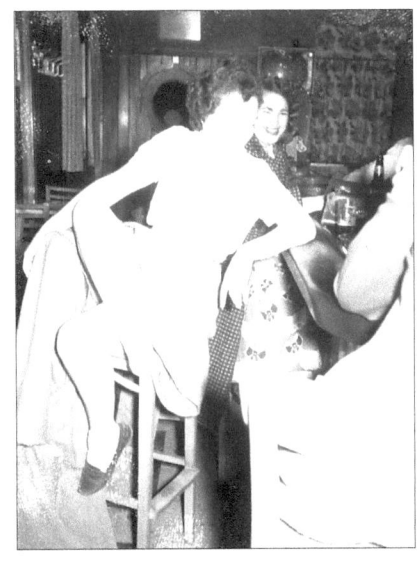

Braciole

INGREDIENTS

BEEF round steak or VEAL	1 lb
(sliced thin, about 10-12 inches in length)	
SALT	1/2 tsp (to taste)
BLACK PEPPER, fresh ground	1/2 tsp
PROSCIUTTO HAM, sliced wafer thin	1 to 2 slices
SPINACH, fresh, chopped	1/2 cup
ASIAGO or PARMIGIANO CHEESE, grated	1/4 cup
PINE NUTS, toasted	1 tbsp
GOLDEN RAISINS	1 tbsp
EGG, hardboiled	1
OLIVE OIL, light	3 tbsps
GARLIC, chopped	3 cloves
SPAGHETTI SAUCE (see recipe on page 34)	1 qt
PARSLEY, fresh, chopped (for garnish)	1 tbsp
ALSO NEEDED: meat mallet, parchment paper, butcher's twine	

PREPARED BY
Lora Lee Ecobelli
Saugerties, NY

PHOTO BY
Lora Lee Ecobelli
Saugerties, NY

(This is for 1 braciole, you can multiply for each roll you make.)

Toast the pine nuts in a heavy skillet over medium heat. They brown quickly, so be careful not to burn them.

Your local butcher might be able to prepare the meat in advance for you. If not, place the meat between two pieces of parchment paper and pound it with a mallet to make it about 1/4" thin. Remove the top paper and sprinkle the meat with salt and pepper. Place a slice of prosciutto ham on the center of the meat, then place the chopped fresh spinach, cheese, pine nuts and raisins and finally the slices of hardboiled egg on top of the ham. Roll up tightly starting at the long end and fold the corners in like a burrito. Tie the braciole tightly with the twine at the two ends and the middle.

Heat the olive oil in a heavy cast iron skillet on medium heat and brown the braciole on all sides. Add the spaghetti sauce and finish cooking slowly for about 40 minutes. To serve, place the braciole on a platter, remove the twine, and slice into rounds at the table. Garnish with the chopped fresh parsley and extra sauce.

Braciole is a scrumptious stuffed meat that is cooked in tomato sauce. It's rolled up like a pinwheel then sliced at the table. Feel free to get creative with this, but here is my recipe based on Laurina's. ~ Lora Lee

I loved watching my grandmother and her friend Anna Pastore talking and laughing as they prepared this dish. As a little kid, it looked like so much fun and I was amazed at how fast they worked. It was almost like an Italian quilting bee. ~Tom

Italian Oven Fried Chicken

INGREDIENTS

ROASTER CHICKEN, whole	1
cut into 8 sections (skin on)	
FLOUR	1/4 cup
YELLOW CORN MEAL, ground fine	1/2 cup
BREAD CRUMBS	1 cup
SALT	1/2 tsp (to taste)
BLACK PEPPER, fresh ground	1/2 tsp (to taste)
ROSEMARY, dried	2 tsp
OREGANO, dried	1/2 tsp
PARSELY, dried	1 tsp
CRUSHED RED PEPPER FLAKES (optional)	1/4 tsp
PARMESAN CHEESE, grated	1/2 cup
EGGS	4
OLIVE OIL, extra virgin	1/4 cup
ROSEMARY, fresh (for garnish)	

IMAGE FROM Vintage Ecobelli's Restaurant Menu

Preheat the oven to 350°. Oil the bottom of a shallow 9" x 13" baking dish. Mix all the spices, dry ingredients and cheese together in a bowl and set aside. Beat the eggs in a separate bowl. Dredge the chicken pieces in breading mixture first, then the eggs, then back into the breading for an extra crispy coating, arranging the chicken pieces on the baking dish. Drizzle the chicken liberally with olive oil and bake uncovered for 1 hour or until chicken is golden brown. Garnish with fresh rosemary. Serve immediately while warm or cold as a delicious picnic food.

In the 1960's our father tried to offer more "American fare" and one of the classics was "Ecobelli's Southern Fried Chicken." That's kind of funny if you think about it because as far south as any of our family had ever been was Southern Italy (Sicily). Never the less, fried chicken was a favorite and many people remember it fondly. I decided to add my slightly more Italian version which is baked instead of fried, but every bit as delicious as our father's. ~ Lora Lee

Lots of good food at an Ecobelli clan picnic.

Madeira

INGREDIENTS

TURKEY, CHICKEN or VEAL cutlets	2 lbs
(sliced thin and cut into 2-inch strips)	
OLIVE OIL, light	4 tbsps
SEASONED FLOUR	1/2 cup
(salt, black pepper, garlic powder, dried parsley)	
BUTTER	4 tbsps
GARLIC, chopped fine	2 cloves
SALT	1/2 tsp (to taste)
BLACK PEPPER, fresh ground	1/2 tsp
ROSEMARY, dried or fresh	1/2 tsp
MUSHROOMS, fresh, sliced	1 cup
MADEIRA WINE	1/2 cup
PARSLEY, fresh, chopped	1 tbsp

PREPARED BY
*Lora Lee Ecobelli
Saugerties, NY*

PHOTO BY
*Lora Lee Ecobelli
Saugerties, NY*

Prepare the meat. In a cast iron skillet, heat the olive oil to medium heat. In a bowl, make the seasoned flour by mixing a pinch of salt, pepper, garlic powder and dried parsley with a 1/2 cup of flour. Dredge the strips of cutlets in the seasoned flour, then brown quickly in the oil. Remove the cutlets, drain, and place them in a baking dish. Keep them warm by placing the dish in the oven on low heat.

In the same skillet, add the butter, garlic, salt, pepper, rosemary and mushrooms, sautéing quickly. Add the wine and simmer for 5 minutes. Return the cutlets to the pan. Spoon the sauce over the cutlets and simmer 5 minutes more. Adjust the seasoning to taste. Garnish with fresh parsley and serve.

Our dad as a teenager (at left) with his best friend, Jeep, a Boston terrier he still talked about way into his 70s. "You know that dog was so smart he could play the piano?" ~ Tom

Chicken Cacciatore

INGREDIENTS

ROASTER CHICKEN, whole	1
cut into 8 sections (skin on)	
OLIVE OIL, light	3 tbsps
SEASONED FLOUR	1/2 cup
(salt and black pepper to taste)	
RED BELL PEPPER, slivered	1 large
GREEN BELL PEPPER, slivered	1 large
ONION, sliced into rings	1 medium
MUSHROOMS, sliced	1-1/2 cups
GARLIC, chopped	3 cloves
SALT	1/2 tsp (to taste)
BLACK PEPPER, fresh ground	1/2 tsp
RED WINE, dry	3/4 cup
TOMATOES, diced, with juice	1 (28 oz) can
CHICKEN BROTH	3/4 cup
CAPERS, drained	3 tbsps
OREGANO, dried	1 tsp
PARSLEY, fresh, chopped	1 tsp
BASIL, fresh, chopped coarse	1/4 cup

PREPARED BY
Lora Lee Ecobelli
Saugerties, NY

PHOTO BY
Lora Lee Ecobelli
Saugerties, NY

Prepare the meat. In a large heavy sauté pan, heat the olive oil to medium heat. In a bowl, make the seasoned flour by mixing a pinch of salt and pepper (to taste) with the 1/2 cup of flour. Dredge the chicken pieces in the seasoned flour, then brown them quickly in the oil, about 5 minutes per side. Transfer the chicken to a plate and set aside.

Add the peppers, onion, mushrooms and garlic to the pan and sauté until the vegetables are just tender. Season with salt and pepper. Add the wine and simmer until reduced by half, about 3 minutes. Add the diced tomatoes, chicken broth, capers, oregano, parsley and basil. Return the chicken pieces to the pan and simmer over medium-low heat until the chicken is cooked through, about 20 minutes for the thighs and legs, and 30 minutes for the breast pieces.

Transfer the chicken to a platter. Spoon off any excess fat from atop the sauce and pour the remaining sauce over the chicken. Garnish with more fresh parsley.

Chicken Cacciatore was a favorite at the restaurant. It is a hearty dish that uses the holy trinity — peppers, onions and mushrooms — and is usually served with roasted potatoes or over pasta. In Italian cacciatore means "hunter style" and is sometimes made with rabbit. I remember Laurina making the rabbit version for my grandfather, but Tom and I steered clear of the bunny stew. Tom kept a pet rabbit on an old pool table in our basement ... sigh ... ~ Lora Lee

Picata

INGREDIENTS

CHICKEN, TURKEY, PORK or VEAL cutlets .... 2 lbs
    (sliced thin and cut into 2-inch strips)
SEASONED FLOUR .... 1/2 cup
    (salt, black pepper, garlic powder, dried rosemary, ground sage)
EGGS 2
PARSLEY, fresh, chopped fine .... 1 tsp
OLIVE OIL, light .... 4 tbsps
LEMON .... 1 large

Prepare the meat. In a bowl, make the seasoned flour by mixing salt, pepper, garlic powder, dried parsley and ground sage (to taste) with a 1/2 cup of flour. Whisk the eggs and parsley in another bowl. In a skillet, heat the olive oil to medium heat.

Dredge the cutlets in the seasoned flour, dip into the egg mixture, then back into the seasoned flour. Fry the cutlets in the oil until lightly browned and crispy.

To serve, garnish with thin lemon slices, sprinkle with fresh-squeezed lemon juice, and top with more fresh parsley.

PREPARED BY
Carolyn Cocca
& Jenny Quirk
Albany, NY

PHOTO BY
Carolyn Cocca
& Jenny Quirk
Albany, NY

This makes a simple and delicate meal. Veal Picata is more traditional, but our contributors used chicken in the picture above. ~ Lora Lee

Scallopino

INGREDIENTS

VEAL, CHICKEN or TURKEY cutlets	2 lbs
(sliced thin and cut into 2-inch strips)	
SEASONED FLOUR	1/2 cup
(salt, black pepper, garlic powder)	
OLIVE OIL, light	4 tbsps
GARLIC, chopped coarse	2 cloves
ONION, sliced thin	1 small
RED BELL PEPPER, slivered	1/2 pepper
GREEN BELL PEPPER, slivered	1/2 pepper
MUSHROOMS, fresh, sliced	1/2 cup
SALT	1/2 tsp (to taste)
BLACK PEPPER, fresh ground	1/2 tsp
RED WINE, dry	1/2 cup
MARINARA SAUCE (see recipe on page 36)	1/2 cup
PARSLEY, fresh, chopped (for garnish)	

PREPARED BY Lora Lee Ecobelli Saugerties, NY

PHOTO BY Lora Lee Ecobelli Saugerties, NY

Prepare the meat. In a bowl, make the seasoned flour by mixing a pinch each of salt, pepper and garlic powder with the 1/2 cup of flour. In a skillet, heat the olive oil to medium.

Dredge the cutlets in the seasoned flour. Brown them quickly in the oil, remove and set aside on a platter lined with paper towels to drain the excess oil. In the same skillet, add the garlic, onion, bell peppers, mushrooms, salt and pepper, sautéing quickly. Add the wine, simmer for 5 minutes, then add the marinara sauce. Return the cutlets back to the skillet. Spoon the sauce over the cutlets and simmer 5 minutes more. Adjust the seasonings to taste. To serve, garnish with fresh parsley.

"The Tam" was famous for scallopino. They were my father's signature dishes. He used mostly veal, but I don't eat veal so I substitute turkey or chicken and it's every bit as good! ~ Lora Lee

Chicken Romano

INGREDIENTS

SEASONED FLOUR	1/2 cup
(salt, black pepper, garlic powder)	
EGGS, beaten	2
PARSLEY, fresh, chopped fine	1 tsp
OLIVE OIL, light	6 tbsps
CHICKEN THIGH, boneless	1
CHICKEN BREAST, boneless	1
BUTTER	4 tbsps
GARLIC, chopped fine	2 cloves
SALT	1/2 tsp (to taste)
BLACK PEPPER, fresh ground, coarse	1/2 tsp (to taste)
ROSEMARY, dried	1 pinch
SAGE, dried ground	1 pinch
PROSCIUTTO HAM, chopped	1/2 cup
or any type HAM or HARD SALAMI	
WHITE WINE, dry	1/2 cup
PEAS, petite, frozen	1/2 cup

PREPARED BY
Lora Lee Ecobelli
Saugerties, NY

PHOTO BY
Lora Lee Ecobelli
Saugerties, NY

In a bowl, make the seasoned flour by mixing salt, pepper and garlic powder (to taste) with a 1/2 cup of flour. Whisk the eggs and parsley in another bowl. In a skillet, heat the olive oil to medium heat.

Dredge the chicken pieces in the seasoned flour, dip into the egg mixture, then back into the seasoned flour. Brown the coated chicken quickly in the oil, remove and set aside. In the same skillet on medium heat, add the butter, garlic, salt, pepper, rosemary and sage, sautéing quickly. Add the ham and white wine. Simmer for 5 minutes.

Return the chicken to the skillet. Spoon the sauce over the chicken and add the peas. Lower the heat and simmer 10 minutes more. Adjust the seasoning to taste. To serve, garnish with more fresh parsley.

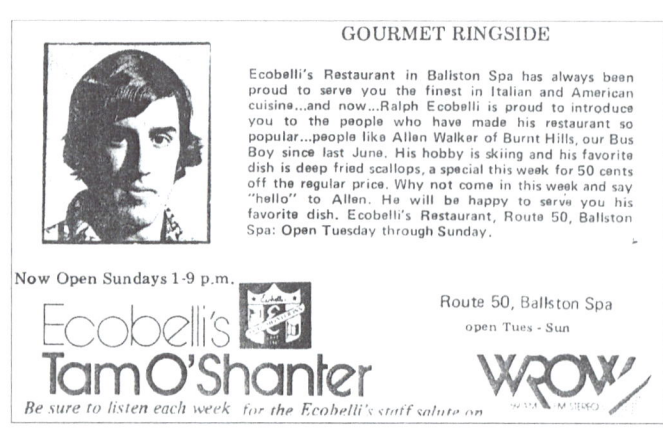

Breaded Cutlets & Parmigiana

BREADED CUTLETS

CHICKEN or VEAL cutlets, sliced thin	2 lbs
BREAD CRUMBS	1 cup
YELLOW CORN MEAL, ground fine	1/2 cup
PARMESAN CHEESE, grated	1/4 cup
GARLIC, chopped fine	2 cloves
OREGANO, dried	1/2 tsp
PARSLEY, fresh, chopped	2 tbsps
SALT	1 tsp (to taste)
BLACK PEPPER, fresh ground, fine	1/2 tsp
EGGS	3
OLIVE OIL, light, or VEGETABLE OIL	1/2 cup

PARMIGIANA

SPAGHETTI SAUCE (see recipe on page 34)	2 cups
PARMESAN CHEESE, grated	1/2 cup
MOZZARELLA CHEESE, grated or sliced	1 cup

*PREPARED BY
Tom Ecobelli
Los Angeles, CA*

*PHOTO BY
Tom Ecobelli
Los Angeles, CA*

In a medium-size bowl, mix the bread crumbs, corn meal, Parmesan cheese, garlic, oregano, parsley, salt and pepper. Whisk the eggs in a separate bowl. In a skillet, heat the oil to medium-high.

Dredge the cutlets in the dry mixture, dip them into the eggs, then back into the dry mixture. Fry the cutlets in the oil on both sides until they are golden brown. To serve the breaded cutlets plain, just remove them from the skillet and let them drain on a platter lined with paper towels. Serve while warm.

For Chicken or Veal Parmigiana: Place the drained cutlets in an oven-proof baking dish with a little of the spaghetti sauce on the bottom. Top the cutlets with additional sauce (to your liking) and sprinkle with Parmesan and mozzarella cheese. Bake at 350° until the cheese is brown and bubbly.

For a kid, there is nothing more satisfying that a chicken or veal cutlet, the Italian version of fried chicken. My brother and I could eat them faster than Laurina could pull them out of the pan. When my own kids wanted Chicken McNuggets like all their friends, I would feed them these instead.

This simple recipe can be eaten plain or used as the base for most parmigiana dishes. When frying cutlets I only use my cast iron pan. Cast iron cookware takes some care, but the benefits are well worth it. It heats up quickly, distributes the heat evenly, and is healthier than nonstick pans. A good set of cast iron fry pans are the only cookware you will ever need and will become a cherished family heirloom. I have Laurina's 12-inch fry pan, and every time I use it I think of her. ~ Lora Lee

Rosemary Chicken

INGREDIENTS

ROASTER CHICKEN, whole	1
or whole chicken cut into 8 sections (skin on)	
LEMON or LIME JUICE, fresh squeezed	2 large
SALT	1/2 tsp (to taste)
BLACK PEPPER, fresh ground	1/2 tsp (to taste)
ROSEMARY, dried (or 1 fresh sprig)	2 tsp
GARLIC, sliced	5 cloves
CAPERS	2 tsp
KALAMATI OLIVES, halved, pitted	1/3 cup
OLIVE OIL, extra virgin	4 tbsps
LEMON, sliced (for garnish)	1

PREPARED BY
Lora Lee Ecobelli
Saugerties, NY

PHOTO BY
Lora Lee Ecobelli
Saugerties, NY

Preheat the oven to 350°. Sprinkle the chicken with the lemon or lime juice, then season all sides with salt, pepper, rosemary and garlic. In an oiled roasting pan, arrange the whole chicken with the breast side up (or the sections with the meat up). Sprinkle the chicken with the olives and capers, and drizzle with the oil. Bake for 1 hour, until chicken is golden brown. Garnish with lemon slices and fresh rosemary sprigs.

Lora Lee as a bay and young girl with Laurina and with her parents, Mary and Ralph.

Easter Lamb

INGREDIENTS

LAMB, boneless leg	3 to 5 lbs
SALT	1 tsp
BLACK PEPPER, fresh ground	1/2 tsp
OREGANO	1 tsp
ROSEMARY, fresh, chopped	1 tsp
1 full sprig additional	
GARLIC, sliced	1 bulb
RED WINE	1-1/2 cups
PARSLEY, fresh, chopped	2 tbsps
FIGS, chopped	1/2 cup
KALAMATA OLIVES, halved	1/4 cup
OLIVE OIL, extra virgin	1/4 cup
FIG PRESERVES (as condiment)	

PREPARED BY
Steve & Diane O'Connor
Loudonville, NY

PHOTO BY
Steve & Diane O'Connor
Loudonville, NY

Lay the lamb flat in a glass baking pan. Season each side with the salt, pepper, oregano, chopped rosemary and half of the garlic. Pour 1 cup of the wine over the meat, cover and refrigerate overnight to marinate.

The next day, preheat the oven to 400°. Take the lamb out of the marinade and lay it fat side down in an oiled roasting pan. Save the marinade. Sprinkle the lamb with the remaining sliced garlic, chopped fresh parsley, figs and olives and roll up jelly-roll fashion, tying tightly with the butcher's twine to secure the filling inside.

Sprinkle the lamb with more black pepper and top with the rosemary sprig. Pour the wine marinade over the lamb, and drizzle with olive oil. Roast the lamb until a meat thermometer reads medium. Let the lamb rest 1/2 hour before slicing. While the meat is resting, deglaze the pan with an additional 1/2 cup of red wine, bring to a boil and then reduce the heat. Adjust salt and pepper to taste. Serve with fig preserves.

Lamb is always served for Easter in Italian households. When I was growing up, it was not uncommon for our grandfather to request Laurina to cook the entire head — eyeballs and all. Okay, okay, I know — purists will say it's a great delicacy, but if you want to traumatize any unwanted guests here's your opportunity. I have spared you the gory details and added a savory and elegant boned leg of lamb that I serve every Easter for my family. And I promise: no one will ever run out of the room screaming. ~ Lora Lee

Lora Lee wasn't the only one freaked out by the lamb's head feast. I remember one Easter where both grandparents were eating it, bibs under their chins and proclaiming, "This is the type of meal you can't order out because you have to dig into it with your hands." They look so nice in this picture, you'd never suspect such behavior … ~ Tom

Roast Chicken and Sausage

INGREDIENTS

CHICKEN (cut into 8 sections)	1 large
ITALIAN SAUSAGE, sweet	1 lb
SPANISH ONION, large, chunked	1
POTATOES, quartered	4
SALT	1/2 tsp (to taste)
BLACK PEPPER, fresh ground	1/2 tsp
GARLIC, slivered	5 cloves
OREGANO	1 tsp
OLIVE OIL, extra virgin	2 tbsp
LEMON JUICE, fresh squeezed	1 large lemon

PREPARED BY
Tom Ecobelli
Los Angeles, CA

PHOTO BY
Tom Ecobelli
Los Angeles, CA

Preheat the oven to 350°. Cut the chicken up into eight sections, leaving the skin on. Arrange the chicken, sausage, onion and potatoes in a large baking pan, with the chicken pieces skin side down. Season everything with the salt, pepper, garlic and oregano. Turn the chicken pieces skin side up, and season again, making sure both sides of everything are seasoned. Drizzle everything with the olive oil and lemon juice. Bake uncovered at 350° for 1 hour until the chicken, sausage and potatoes are browned and fork tender.

Everyone made this in our family. It was a standard recipe, but I think our father's version was the best because he used his homemade sausage. It brings back warm memories of home, and when I close my eyes I can still smell the savory aroma. ~ Lora Lee

I have to disagree with Lora Lee. I think Laurina's first-born child, our Aunt Joanne, was the best cook of this dish. She'd always make a giant pan of it whenever we'd visit. It smelled so good I was tempted to sneak a peek as it was cooking, but a certain someone always gave me the evil eye before I could. Aunt Joanne had a little Chihuahua named Peanut that used to have a bed right next to the stove. Those lips would curl, and look out! Peanut was a nippy little thing and I kept my distance until mealtime. ~ Tom

Joanne D'Carlo

FAMILY SPECIALS

TOM'S OLIVES	0.70
ALANA'S SOUTHERN ITALIAN SWEET POTATOES	0.72
DAVID'S LA BOHEME SURVIVAL OMELET	0.73
BRAMRAM'S RAVIOLI WITH SAGE BUTTER	0.74
ADAM'S OCTOPUS	0.76
LEO'S BURIED CHICKEN	0.77

ANNOUNCING
ecobelli's
GOURMET SPECIALS
OFFERED ON THE
DESIGNATED DAYS DURING
SEPTEMBER-MAY
8.95

Tom's Olives

INGREDIENTS

OLIVES, natural black or green, fresh, hand picked	5 lbs
KOSHER SALT, coarse	10 to 15 lbs
OLIVE OIL, extra virgin	1 liter
LEMON, large	2
ORANGE, large	2
ROSEMARY, fresh	1 bunch
GARLIC, whole cloves, peeled	2 bulbs
GLASS JARS, 8 oz size, with lids	1 doz

PREPARED BY
Tom Ecobelli
Los Angeles, CA

PHOTO BY
Tom Ecobelli
Los Angeles, CA

If you're lucky enough to be able to pick fresh olives from a tree, gather 5 pounds and wash them thoroughly. Allow them to dry. If they are green and you want to speed the process, you can make a small slit with a paring knife into each olive. This will allow the salt to permeate faster.

In a clean covered container (preferably glass, I used plastic) cover the olives completely with the salt. Twice a day give the container a good shake to distribute the salt evenly and to rough up the skin of the olives. When the salt becomes damp (usually after 5 days) sift out the olives and replace with fresh salt, making sure to completely cover the olives.

Continue shaking twice a day (approx. every 12 hours) and replace the salt when it becomes damp, until the skin on the olives shrivels and they look like plump raisins. According to your altitude and local weather conditions, this whole process could take up to 2 months or more. Mine took about 65 days.

Once the olives are shriveled, give them a taste. If the bitterness has subsided you're good to proceed to the next step. When fully cured they will have a mild bitterness, but they will be inedibly bitter if they're not ready.

Wash and dry the dozen 8-ounce glass jars. (If you use larger jars, increase the following ingredients accordingly).

Zest the skin of 1 lemon and 1 orange. Peel and slice the rind of 1 lemon and 1 orange, removing as much of the white membrane as possible. Into the bottom of each 8-ounce glass jar, place: a 1/2 teaspoon (combined) of the orange and lemon zest, 2 lemon rind and 2 orange rind slices, 1 sprig of rosemary and 1 clove of garlic. Add the olives to just below the rim of the jar. Cover the olives with the olive oil and seal the jar with the lid.

Let the olives marinate for 3 to 4 days. Invert the jar occasionally to mix the oil and seasonings. Once the olives are fully marinated they'll have a wonderful citrus, rosemary and garlic flavor. Add them to your salads or enjoy them from the jar. If refrigerated, the olives will last up to 3 weeks.

Olive trees near Tom Ecobelli's house.

I live in a suburban area on the outskirts of Los Angeles. Many of the streets are lined with breezy, tall olive trees with silvery green leaves and gnarled trunks. Every summer to early fall I noticed the sidewalks underneath them stained with crushed, black fruits, kind of like what we have in the northeast underneath Mulberry trees. I was surprised to realize no one ever harvested the fruit ... until I moved into the neighborhood. I had a distant memory of our grandmother Laurina telling me she used to salt-cure anchovies and olives when she was a child. Unfortunately I couldn't find her recipe, but the process is very simple. Olives are inedible before curing and the recipe is time consuming, but it's fun and anyone can do it. ~ Tom

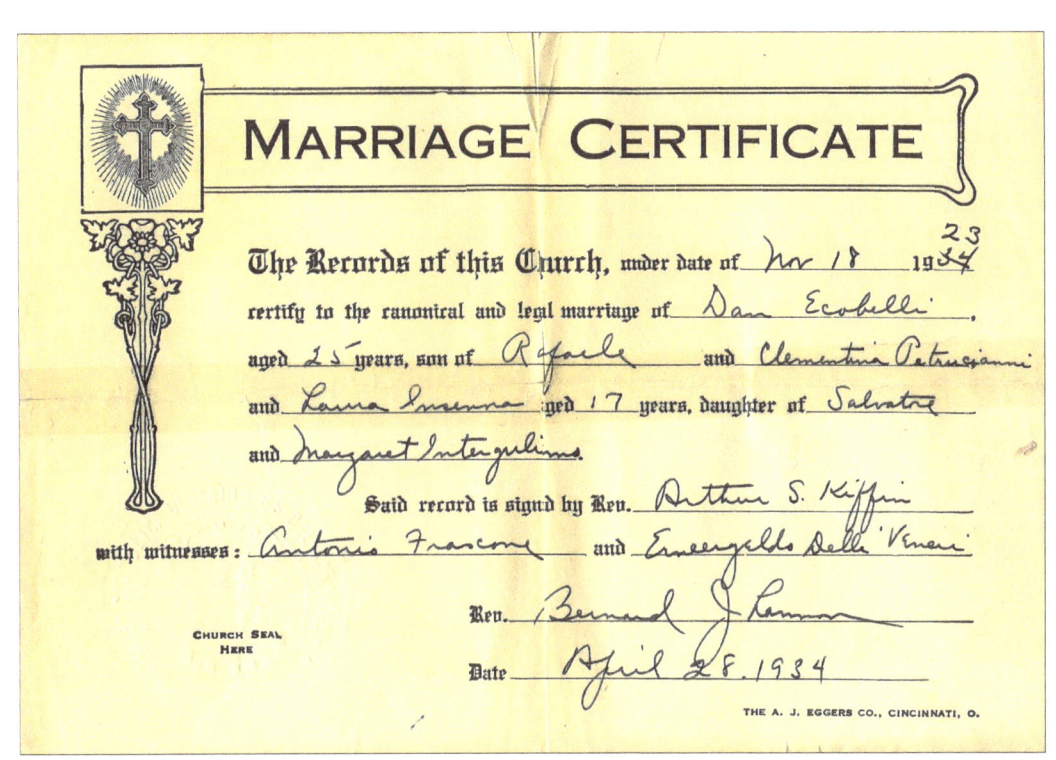

Alana's Southern Italian Sweet Potatoes

This is my daughter Alana's favorite recipe and she always makes it on Thanksgiving. It's an Italian twist to a Southern sweet potato salad and guaranteed to be a favorite in your household too. ~ Lora Lee

INGREDIENTS

SWEET POTATOES, peeled, cubed	4-1/2 cups
OLIVE OIL, extra virgin	3 tbsps
KOSHER SALT	1/2 tsp
BLACK PEPPER, fresh ground	1/2 tsp
HONEY	2 tbsps
APPLE CIDER VINEGAR	1/4 cup
ROSEMARY, fresh, chopped	2 tsps
GARLIC, chopped	2 cloves
CRANBERRIES, dried	1/2 cup
PECANS, toasted	1/2 cup
RED ONION, small, chopped fine	1/2 onion

PREPARED BY Alana Amram Brooklyn, NY

PHOTO BY Alana Amram Brooklyn, NY

Toast the pecans on an oiled baking sheet while the oven preheats to 450°. Toast the pecans until they are golden and crunchy, but be sure not to burn them.

In a large mixing bowl, toss the sweet potatoes in the olive oil, salt and pepper. Place the potatoes on a lightly-oiled baking sheet, and bake for about 35 minutes, or until lightly browned and fork tender. In a large mixing bowl, whisk together the oil, onions, honey, vinegar, rosemary, garlic, cranberries and pecans. Toss in the baked potatoes and coat them well. Let the salad cool before serving.

I have had many jobs to support my real job of playing music. I have worked in the bar and restaurant world on and off for 15 years. In between tours and recording I could always find bar or kitchen work. Due to my upbringing, I feel most comfortable in a kitchen or on stage. I first made up this recipe after a trip down South, where sweet potatoes are a proud staple of Southern American Cuisine. This colorful, sweet and savory dish makes a great companion to braised meat, and it's vegan too. It is a pretty and healthy alternative to the marshmallow-covered Thanksgiving mush! It has become a staple at all our family meals. ~ Alana

Laurina holding Alana. She would be proud her great-grandchildren are becoming such creative cooks.

Alana has a successful music career with her band "Alana Amram & the Rough Gems." Photo by Paul Nemirah Collins.

David's La Boheme Survival Omelet

We're so proud to have David Amram composing the score for our film Chickadee (see page 100), based on Laurina's life. Besides us, David is the only other person working on the project that knew and loved her. Thank you, David. ~ Lora Lee and Tom

INGREDIENTS

EGGS	4
SALT	1/4 tsp (to taste)
BLACK PEPPER, fresh ground	1/4 tsp (to taste)
THYME, dried	pinch
BUTTER, unsalted	1 tbsp
ONION, medium, diced	1
GARLIC, minced	1 clove
MUSHROOMS, sliced	1/4 cup
CHERRY TOMATOES	1/4 cup
SWISS CHEESE	4 slices
PARSLEY, fresh, chopped	1 tsp
SOUR CREAM (for garnish)	1 tbsp
MANGO PEACH SALSA (for garnish)	1 tbsp

Photo by Adira Amram.

In a bowl, whisk together the eggs, salt, pepper and thyme. Melt the butter in a pan on medium heat and sauté the onion, garlic, mushrooms and tomatoes until tender.

Pour in the eggs and let them set for a moment. Then jiggle the pan to loosen from the bottom. When the eggs are just slightly firm, top them with the Swiss Cheese slices. Cover the pan just long enough for the cheese to melt. Remove the omelet gently from the pan and transfer to a serving plate.

To serve, sprinkle the omelet with the fresh parsley, and garnish with sour cream and mango peach salsa on the side as condiments. Accompany with toasted English muffins.

In 1951, I was listening to a recording of Puccinni's La Boheme with Bidou Sayou singing the role of Mimi. I decided to make an omelet as I imagined the characters in the opera would make, creatively combining whatever was in the ice box at the moment. I never dared to make it for anyone in the Ecobelli family, since not only Grandma Laurina — but EVERYONE in the family — was an incredible cook in their own right. To me, they were equal in ability, imagination, nuance and flair to the opera singers in that great recording I had listened to decades before when I first drafted this dish. "Don't worry David," said Laurina, when I told her of my insecurity as a chef. "It's just like music. You have to learn a way to do it, but it's always a little different every time. Just cook with your heart the way you make music, and it will be good." She was a world-class cook, but like all great artists, she fostered confidence and creativity in others. ~ David Amram

Left to right: Larry Rivers, Jack Kerouac, David Amram, Allen Ginsberg and Gregory Corso (in white hat), 1959, on break while making the Beat film "Pull My Daisy." Photo by John Cohen, courtesy of David Amram.

Bramram's Ravioli with Sage Butter

RAVIOLI DOUGH

See the recipe for Ravioli Dough on page 44.

MUSHROOM FILLING

BUTTER	1/4 cup
GARLIC, pressed	1 clove
MUSHROOMS, any variety, chopped fine	1 lb
PARSLEY, fresh, chopped fine	1 tsp
SAGE, crushed	1 tsp
SALT	1/2 tsp (to taste)
BLACK PEPPER, fresh ground	1/2 tsp
WHITE WINE, dry	splash
HEAVY CREAM	3 tbsps

*PREPARED BY
Adira Amram &
Bram Muller
New York, NY*

*PHOTO BY
Bram Muller
New York, NY*

SAGE BUTTER

BUTTER	1/4 cup
FLOUR, all-purpose	2 tsps
HEAVY CREAM	1/4 cup
SALT	to taste
BLACK PEPPER, fresh ground	to taste
SAGE, dried or fresh	1 tsp

While your ravioli dough is resting, prepare your filling.

In a pan, melt the butter and sauté the garlic and mushrooms. Add the parsley, sage and salt and pepper to taste. Add the wine and simmer slowly for a few minutes. Add the heavy cream and simmer more to let the liquid reduce. (The mushrooms should not have a lot of liquid.)

With a floured rolling pin or a pasta machine, roll out two thin (less than 1/8 inch), long sheets of pasta. With a rolling pin you can make bigger sheets (about 12-inch squares) than with a machine, but it is harder work by hand. Use more flour if needed to keep the sheets from sticking.

Drop about 1 tablespoon of the filling mixture onto the dough, and continue in a grid pattern about 4 inches apart. Brush a little water around each dollop of filling.

Cover the pasta sheet and filling with the other sheet of pasta. Using a 2-inch ravioli press, cut out the individual ravioli squares and remove them. Pinch the edges together with a fork and dredge the ravioli in flour. Place the ravioli on parchment paper, making sure they are individually separated. Let them dry for about 1 hour.

To cook your ravioli, bring salted water to a boil in a large pot. Cook the ravioli for just a few minutes; they will float to the surface when they are done. Drain well. While the water is coming to a boil, prepare the ingredients for the Sage Butter, which you can make while you cook your ravioli.

On med/low heat, melt the butter in a small sauce pan, add the flour, whisking together to make a light roux, do not brown, add cream and seasonings until the sauce thickens about 5 minutes. Dress the ravioli with the Sage Butter and garnish with fresh parsley.

This is a great recipe from my daughter Adira and her Dutch husband Bram. They love to experiment with traditional recipes and are both avid mushroom hunters. They served this delicate and delicious ravioli as an appetizer one recent Christmas day. It was such a big hit it has now become a part of our yearly holiday celebration. ~ Lora Lee

Laurina with Adira.

Adira and Bram. Photo by Tom Ecobelli.

Some wild mushrooms gathered by Adira and Bram for this recipe. Photos by Bram Muller.

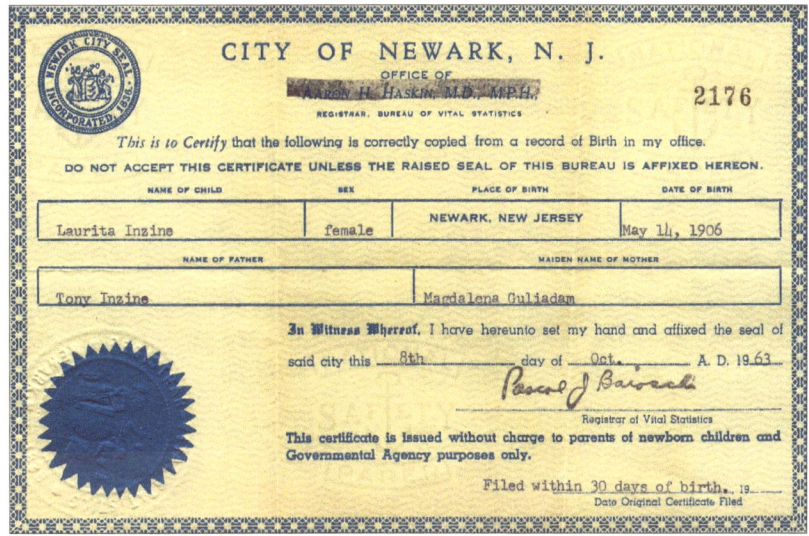

Adam's Octopus

INGREDIENTS

WATER	2 cups
OCTOPUS, cleaned, tentacles sliced	1 - 2 lbs
RED ONION, small, chopped	1
TOMATO, small, chopped	1
PARSLEY, fresh, chopped	1 tbsp
OREGANO	1/2 tsp
LEMON JUICE, fresh squeezed	3 lemons
OLIVE OIL, extra virgin	3 tbsps
SALT	1/2 tsp (to taste)
BLACK PEPPER, fresh ground	1/2 tsp
ROMAINE LETTUCE	

PREPARED BY
Tom Ecobelli
Los Angeles, CA

PHOTO BY
Tom Ecobelli
Los Angeles, CA

Prepare the octopus. In a large enough pot of salted, boiling water, blanch the octopus for 5 minutes. Remove from the pot and let cool in a mixing bowl. Add the remaining ingredients and toss together well. Let the octopus marinate in the refrigerator for at least 4 hours before serving over a bed of lettuce.

My son Adam discovered octopus when he went diving off the coast of Italy. It is eaten raw there right on the beach in a sort of Italian ceviche with lemon juice. After the octopus is caught, it is pounded on the rocks to tenderize it. According to common wisdom, the citric acid in the lemon "cooks" the octopus — partially or completely, depending on how long it is marinated. But the lemon juice does not kill bacteria as well as heat does, so it's important to start with the freshest fish possible. If you are squeamish about using raw octopus, you can blanch it quickly for about 5 minutes in salted, boiling water. Do not overcook it or it will be rubbery.
~ Lora Lee

Adam hunts his octopus.

Leo's Buried Chicken

Lora Lee's late husband, Leo Burmester, was a brilliant actor, poet, musician and sculptor. He was a huge, booming, creative spirit with a legendary gusto for life. Leo was so moved by Laurina's life story that he became a founding producer of our film Chickadee (see page 100) and was instrumental in getting the project off the ground. ~ Tom

INGREDIENTS

ROASTER CHICKEN	1 large
APPLES, chopped	1
CRANBERRIES, dried	1/2 cup
PECANS or WALNUTS, chopped	1/4 cup
OLIVE OIL	2 tbsps
SAGE, fresh	1 tsp
MINT, fresh	1 tsp
SALT	1/2 tsp
BLACK PEPPER, fresh ground	1/2 tsp
CAJUN SEASONING	1/2 tsp
ONION, chopped small	1
BUTTER	1 stick
GARLIC POWDER	1 tsp

Dig a hole in your backyard (or your neighbor's) that is deep and wide enough to cover both the chicken and some coals. Pile up some hardwood in the hole and get a good fire going.

Mix the apples, cranberries and nuts together in a bowl to make a stuffing, and stuff the chicken. Put the chicken on a large sheet of aluminum foil. Cover the outside of the chicken with olive oil and season liberally with the sage, mint, salt, pepper, Cajun seasoning and garlic powder. Sprinkle on the chopped onion. Place pads of butter on the chicken wherever they will fit. Close the aluminum foil tightly around the chicken then wrap it entirely in five more layers of foil.

When the wood has burned down to red-hot coals, carefully shovel a layer of dirt over them. Place the foil-wrapped chicken on the dirt layer, and cover it with more dirt.

Let the chicken sit for 1 1/2 hours. Remove the layer of dirt, being careful not to puncture the foil. With oven mitts, remove the chicken from the pit. (You might want to use fireplace gloves to remove both the dirt and the chicken.) Remove the foil from the chicken, and dig in! The chicken will either be falling-off-the-bone delicious, or completely incinerated beyond recognition.

Leo and I always had a backyard campfire where we sat around, played music and told stories with our combined Brady Bunch-like families. Leo would make this recipe and you never knew how it was going to come out. So just to be safe, he would set off a few fireworks and make sure there was plenty of beer so nobody would complain too much if it was a disaster. As Leo would say, "Put on a wild hair and give life a try!" So I encourage you to take a risk and be adventurous. Though not anywhere close to a traditional Italian recipe, Laurina would have approved of this dish because she was the same kind of spontaneous cook Leo was. And believe me, this recipe gives a new meaning to "trial by fire." More times than not, it was more like a cremation than a burial, but when it did come out right it was truly delicious. ~ Lora Lee

An Ecobelli Family Sampler

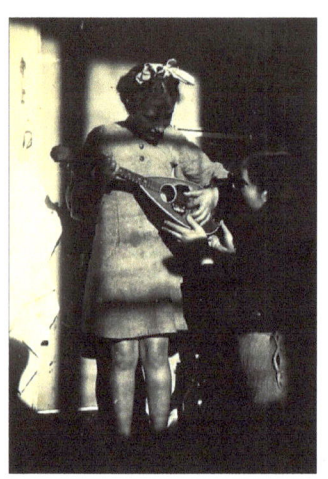

A sampling of photos from the Ecobelli family collection.

DESSERTS

AUNT ANNA'S CHRISTMAS COOKIES	0.80
LEMON ICE	0.81
PIGNOLI COOKIES	0.82
LEMON RICOTTA EASTER PIE	0.83
AMARETTO CHEESECAKE	0.84
E-WANDS	0.85

The Freddie Freihofer Show was a popular Schenectady-area children's television show in the '50's and '60's. It was sponsored by the Freihofer Baking company, which is famous in upstate New York for its delicious cakes and cookies. It was hosted by Freddie Freihofer himself (a giant rabbit) and the cartoonist Jim Fisk and his signature squiggle drawings. The show featured music and stories and, of course, lots of goodies. Many area children appeared on the TV show on their birthdays, including yours truly, and each kid was given their very own birthday cake. It was my first venture into the world of show biz singing the Freddie Freihofer song — but I got into trouble for sticking my fingers into my cake to taste it!

Ecobelli's was a huge supporter of our local businesses. Every Saturday morning the Freihofer truck would pull up to the restaurant and deliver boxes of Chocolate Chip and Black-Eyed Susan cookies. Laurina would buy boxes of them to give to the children of her employees and to her favorite customers. ~ Lora Lee (front row, second from left)

Freddie Freihofer Song

Freddie, Freihofer we think you're swell.
Freddie, we love the stories you tell.
We love your cookies, your cakes and your pies,
We love the way you roll those funny bunny eyes.
Freddie, we're ready, we're waiting for you,
Freddie, we love all the things that you do.
We love your cookies your bread and your cakes.
We love everything Freddie Freihofer bakes.

Aunt Anna's Christmas Cookies

COOKIE DOUGH

SUGAR	1 cup
FLOUR	5 cups
SALT	1/4 tsp
BAKING POWDER	2 tsp
EGGS, beaten well	6
BUTTER, melted	1/2 cup
MILK	4 tbsps
VANILLA	1 tsp
LEMON FLAVORING or ANISETTE	1/2 tsp

COOKIE GLAZE

BUTTER	1/3 cup
POWDERED SUGAR	2 cups
VANILLA	2 tsps
LEMON FLAVORING or ANISETTE	1 tsp
MILK	2 - 4 tsps
COLORED SPRINKLES (optional)	1 tsp

PREPARED BY Chelsea Lauber & Boo Boo Kitty Los Angeles, CA

PHOTO BY Chelsea Lauber Los Angeles, CA

(makes about 2 dozen cookies)

Preheat the oven to 400°. In a large mixing bowl, mix sugar, flour, salt and baking powder together. Whisk the eggs in a separate bowl then add them to the dry ingredients along with the butter, milk, vanilla and flavoring. Mix well, then knead together with your hands like bread dough. Grease your hands and pinch off about 1 tablespoon of dough. Roll it into a 2-inch rope and wind it like a pinwheel. Repeat until the dough is gone. Bake the cookies on a greased cookie sheet for 10 minutes at 400°.

For the glaze, heat the butter in a small sauce pan over low heat until melted. Stir in the powdered sugar, vanilla, flavoring and milk. Stir the glaze until it gets smooth. Brush the cookies with the glaze while the cookies are still hot. Top with the colored sprinkles (optional).

These are more like a biscuit than a cookie and are great with coffee on Christmas morning. Our Aunt Anna always made piles of them and sometimes she substituted anisette for the lemon flavoring. ~ Lora Lee

A photo of me bribing Aunt Anna for more of her Christmas cookies. She seems a little skeptical of my intentions. ~ Tom

Lemon Ice

INGREDIENTS

WATER, boiling	4 cups
SUGAR	1 1/2 cups
LEMON JUICE, fresh squeezed	1 cup
LEMON PEEL, grated	1 tbsp

Boil some water and measure out 4 cups. Dissolve the sugar in the boiling water, and let the sugar water cool. Add the lemon juice and the grated peel. Freeze in a metal tray, stirring the crystals every 10 minutes as it becomes slushy. Do not let it freeze solid. After about 1 hour, scoop the ice treat into cups to serve.

To make other flavors of Italian Ice, you can substitute orange, lime, grape or cherry juice for the lemon juice.

PREPARED BY
Tom Ecobelli
Los Angeles, CA

PHOTO BY
Tom Ecobelli
Los Angeles, CA

We rarely had desserts as a kid. Cakes and pies were served for special occasions but for the most part desserts were only served on holidays. In the summers however, Laurina always made us homemade lemon ice. It's fun and easy to prepare, refreshing, and just as good as ice cream on a hot day!

The picture below was taken when I was about nine years old and I put on a Dracula play in our basement. Laurina made lemon ice to be served as a refreshment during intermission. When word spread, all the kids in the neighborhood showed up. I wish I could say it was because of my great acting and directing, but I know better. To this day, some of my friends still talk about the "lemon ice play." ~ Lora Lee

I was only four when this picture was taken, but I still remember that wonderful lemon ice. Out of all the dishes our father served in the restaurant, surprisingly, this was one of the items he was most proud of. ~ Tom

Pignoli Cookies

INGREDIENTS

PIGNOLI (pine nuts)	8 oz
ALMOND PASTE	8 oz
GRANULATED SUGAR	1/2 cup
POWDERED SUGAR	1/2 cup
FLOUR, all-purpose	1/4 cup
EGG WHITES, beaten lightly	2 med. eggs

(makes about 2 dozen cookies)

Preheat oven to 300°. Grease two baking sheets or line them with parchment paper. Place the pine nuts into a bowl.

In a food processor, break up the almond paste into small pieces. Add the two sugars and the flour and pulse together. Once the mixture is finely ground, begin to add the egg whites a little at a time, just until the dough comes together.

Using a spoon and wet hands, scoop a small spoonful of the dough, and place this into the bowl of pine nuts. Roll the dough around until it is lightly coated with the nuts, and place it on the prepared baking sheet. Continue forming the cookies in this manner, placing them 2 inches apart on the baking sheet.

Bake the cookies at 300° for 20-25 minutes, and allow them to cool. Dust them lightly with powdered sugar before serving.

PREPARED BY
Lora Lee Ecobelli
Saugerties, NY

PHOTO BY
Lora Lee Ecobelli
Saugerties, NY

No special occasion would be complete without these delicious cookies. They are always served at weddings, where they are mixed with Jordan almonds for good luck. Guests would wrap them in napkins to take home as a delicious remembrance of the day. ~ Lora Lee

Lemon Ricotta Easter Pie

INGREDIENTS

BUTTER	1 tbsp
ALMONDS, ground	3/4 cup
FLOUR	1/4 cup
BUTTER, room temperature	3/4 cup
SUGAR	1 cup
EGGS, separated	4
RICOTTA CHEESE	3/4 cup
LEMON ZEST	1 tsp
LEMON JUICE	1/4 cup
CONFECTIONERS' SUGAR (for dusting)	1/4 cup

Preheat oven to 325° degrees. Grease an 8-inch springform pan with the tablespoon of butter. Line the bottom of the pan with parchment paper. In a bowl, combine the ground almonds with the flour and set aside.

Using an electric mixer, beat the room-temperature butter with the sugar until light and fluffy. Separate the eggs and add the egg yolks. (Save the egg whites in a separate bowl.) Continue beating with the mixer until well combined. Add the ricotta cheese, lemon zest and lemon juice. Beat until combined. With a spatula, fold in the almond-flour mixture. Set aside.

In a clean bowl, beat the egg whites with the mixer until stiff peaks form. With a spatula, gently fold the egg whites into the cake mixture. Pour the entire mixture into the spring-form pan.

Bake for 45 minutes at 325° until the top is lightly browned and the pie is still slightly soft in the center. Remove the pie from the oven and allow it to cool in the pan. Just before serving, dust the top with confectioners' sugar, and release it from the pan.

PREPARED BY
Peter Marino
Saratoga Springs, NY

PHOTO BY
Peter Marino
Saratoga Springs, NY

I don't quite remember where or when this photo was taken, probably at some department store. Obviously, it's around Easter time, and though I look like I'm interested in what the Easter Bunny has to say, I'm sure all I was really worried about was where the candy was hidden. ~ Tom

Amaretto Cheesecake

CRUST

GRAHAM CRACKERS, crushed	2 1/2 cups
BUTTER, melted	2/3 cup

CHEESECAKE

CREAM CHEESE	32 oz
EGGS	6
SUGAR	1 1/2 cups
BUTTER, melted	1/2 cup
VANILLA	1 tbsp
LEMON JUICE	1 tbsp
SOUR CREAM	16 oz
ALMOND EXTRACT	1 tbsp
ORANGE EXTRACT	1 tbsp
AMARETTO LIQUEUR	1/4 cup

PREPARED BY
Peter Marino
Saratoga Springs, NY

PHOTO BY
Peter Marino
Saratoga Springs, NY

To make the crust, combine the ingredients and mix thoroughly. In a 10-inch springform pan, press the crust mixture evenly into the bottom of the pan and about 1 inch up the sides. Place the pan in the refrigerator while you make the filling.

Preheat the oven to 350°. For the filling, place the cream cheese in a bowl and using an electric mixer, mix on "cream" setting until smooth. Add the eggs and beat until they are well incorporated. Add all the remaining filling ingredients and blend until smooth. Pour the filling into the spring-form pan.

Place the spring-form pan into a roasting pan that is half full of hot water. Bake at 350° for 1 hour or until the center is set. Remove the spring-form pan from the roasting pan and place it on a rack to allow the cake to cool in the pan. The cheesecake can be refrigerated in the pan until serving time. Release it from the pan before serving.

In the early 1970's our family went through what Tom and I call the "cheesecake phase." It started with our mother experimenting and quickly became a competition that involved the entire family. They each had what they thought was the "best-and-only" recipe, and the only one worth preserving. I found this in the family recipe book and to tell the truth I can't remember whose it was. But in someone's mind it was a world record. ~ Lora Lee

E-Wands

INGREDIENTS

BUTTER, unsalted, room temperature	4 tbsps
EGGS	3 large
VANILLA EXTRACT	1 tsp
FLOUR	1-3/4 cups
BAKING POWDER	3 tsps
SALT	1/4 tsp
VEGETABLE OIL (for frying)	1 cup
CONFECTIONERS' SUGAR (for dusting)	

*PREPARED BY
Chelsea Lauber
& Boo Boo Kitty
Los Angeles, CA*

*PHOTO BY
Chelsea Lauber
Los Angeles, CA*

(makes about 40 cookies)

Using an electric mixer, beat together the butter, eggs, and vanilla. On low speed, gradually add 1 cup of the flour, the baking powder and the salt. When it forms into a ball, transfer the dough to a well-floured surface and knead in the remaining flour with your hands. The dough should be smooth and elastic. Add additional flour if the dough is too sticky.

Divide the dough in half. With a rolling pin, roll out one piece into a rectangular shape about 1/8" thick. Using a pastry cutter, cut the dough into strips about 4" x 2" in size. Cut a small slit in the center of each strip. Take one end of the strip and pull it through the slit in the center. This will give you a bow-tie shape. Continue rolling and shaping all the dough in the same manner.

Heat the vegetable oil in a deep fryer to 375°. Drop 4 or 5 of the e-wands into the oil; fry just a handful of cookies at a time so they are not crowded. Fry for 1-2 minutes, turning them often with a slotted spoon, just until they are lightly browned on both sides. Remove the cookies from the oil with a slotted spoon and transfer them to a platter lined with paper towels to drain. When cooled, dust them with confectioners' sugar before serving.

Dainty strips of sweetened, fried dough are eaten throughout Italy and are known by a variety of names. Laurina called these "e-wands." They were crunchy and delicious and it was impossible to eat just one of them. They don't keep well, so you'd better have a party! ~ Lora Lee

Laurina in Dan's hometown of Benevento, Italy. Benevento is known as the haunted city of witches, similar to Salem in Massachusetts.

Ecobelli's At Large

Ecobelli's was active in both the local community and the restaurant industry. Ralph Ecobelli was ahead of the times with innovations such as "smoke-free" nights and gift certificates.

CUSTOMER COMMENTS

RESTAURANT REVIEWS	0.88
STAFF MEMORIES	0.89
WORD OF MOUTH	0.92

WORLD FAMOUS RESTAURANTS INTERNATIONAL

NEWS RELEASE

FOR IMMEDIATE RELEASE:

RESTAURANT AWARDED INTERNATIONAL HONOR

The _Ecobelli's Tam O'Shanter Inn_ of _Ballston Spa_ has been awarded a special honor by being invited to membership in World Famous Restaurants International.

As a fraternal membership, owners and managers of the finer restaurants in the world have an opportunity for goodwill, to exchange ideas and to have their restaurant publicized on an international basis.

Selections of unusual, quaint and distinctive dining establishments are made on the recommendation of leading newspapers and editors and by the judgement of the Executive Committee.

An International Directory of all member restaurants will be available soon to travel agencies, clubs, organizations and to the general public, who may wish to visit these attractive restaurants, wherever they travel in the world.

The _Ecobelli's Tam O'Shanter_ Restaurant was established in _1947_ is operated by _the Ecobelli Family_ and is noted for its _Italian American Cuisine._

Restaurant Reviews

The name is strange, but the menu is good at Ecobelli's

Ecobelli's: Oldie, mostly goodie

By STEVE BARNES
Arts Editor

BALLSTON SPA — Ecobelli's Restaurant is a time warp.

Merely stepping through the doors of this area institution sends the mind back. Imagine what the veal parmigiana — breaded, baked beneath a mozzarella blanket, puddled with the ever-present red sauce — will do to the memory and senses. One bite and surely you'll feel transported to an era long gone.

The restaurant has been pretty much the same for the 22 years since owner (and sometime chef) Anthony Iaia took over. And old-timers remember Ralph Ecobelli, who put his name on this classically conventional place for Northern Italian food, located on Route 50 south of the village of Ballston Spa, when he opened it in 1956.

Even the menu is a constant. Matt Paston, chef on and off for the past dozen years, says the restaurant's 60 offerings (more than 50 of which are entrees) have been on the menu virtually unchanged for the past seven years. He and Iaia sat down in the early '90s to review the food lineup, but decided that there was hardly anything that didn't sell.

Not are the regular customers have clear favorites — besides, of course, dishes based on veal, which is hand-cut on the premises (a whole leg is broken down into scallopini, cutlets and the familiar chunks for veal and peppers and veal cacciatore).

Admittedly, the age is starting to show in some places. Furthermore, diners looking for something contemporary cooking or a post-millennial melding of cultures and cuisines need not bother to stop in.

REVIEW

ECOBELLI'S RESTAURANT, 1475 Schenectady-Saratoga Road (Route 50), Ballston Spa

Style: Classic Northern Italian

Strengths: Traditional preparation; garlic rolls; old-fashioned atmosphere

Weaknesses: Heavy cream sauces

Must-have dishes: Veal Ala Anthony; Shrimp Fra Diavolo

Prices: 5-$15 (entrees $7.50-$13.95; most $11-$15)

Details: Open for lunch 11:30 a.m.-2 p.m. Tuesdays through Fridays; for dinner, 4-10 p.m. Tuesdays through Thursdays, 5-11 p.m. Fridays and Saturdays, 3-9 p.m. Sundays. Handicapped-accessible. Smoking in bar and separate dining area. Visa, Mastercard, Discover cards accepted. Reservations encouraged on weekends.

Info: 885-5900

SHRIMP MARSALA is part of the extensive menu at Ecobelli's.

nuances of the veal. Regrettably, the scallops of beef were over-done in our serving, which detracted from the exceptional entree. The mushroom sauce, with a gentle beef stock and Worcestershire ...

its with the Italian American community around Ballston Spa.

My regular dining companion, John, selected as his entree Veal Ala Anthony ($16.95), a dish that made up for its standard ham-provolone-and-mushroom accompaniments with wild execution.

"There are a few little things they could do to make things so much better," John observed. He pointed to the wine glasses, the diameter of which made it difficult to sip. They were too small for our noses — pretty normal noses, unexceptional in size in either direction — to fit inside, too large to slip below the nose, like it soda bottle. And so there we sat, vexed by wine glasses, trying to sip the requisite Chianti ($15.95) out of the sides our of our mouths.

The salad bar showed a lack of attention. The ice had melted, leaving the sliced vegetables — bell peppers, carrots, celery, as expected — bobbing in lukewarm water. And both the cream sauce on ...

Ecobelli's Tam O'Shanter offers best Italian-American menus

The Tam O'Shanter Inn, just south of the village, is retaining its reputation for finest Italian food in the area. The reason lies in the owners, Daniel Ecobelli and his son, Ralph, who purchased the establishment from Angus and Peggy Heggie in 1947. The partnership is celebrating its 20th year of sound business.

Since the name "Tam O'Shanter" came along with the business and since the "Tam" was well-known the Ecobelli's decided to keep it. Today, the restaurant is known as Ecobelli's Tam O'Shanter. Dan has since retired from the active business but lends a hand now and then and is still on the advisory committee, his son says.

The Ecobellis have traveled extensively in Europe especially in Italy, from Sicily to the Alps. Wherever they went they have collected unusual recipes which makes their bill of fare interesting as well as delicious.

An example of the variety is seen in the different scallopino dishes, unusual chicken dishes, marvelous lasagne, manicotti and an antipasto which is a work of art. Ecobelli's are hosts to clubs, banquets and wedding parties as well as regular guests. The banquet menus are extensive and contain a variety of American dishes as well. On holidays, hundreds head for dinner at Ecobelli's. The atmosphere is congenial and food superb.

In its progress report, Ecobelli's increased the size of the kitchen in 1952 to meet its growing needs. In 1954 they added to the dining room and two years later, another section was added to the kitchen.

Major remodeling and renovation in 1961 was carried out in all areas, kitchen, dining and banquet rooms and the bar. This included decor changes and an increase in seating capacity of all facilities.

The Tam menus have been written up in such magazines as the Gourmet and Duncan Hines. Many of its recipes will be found in leading cook books.

DAN ECOBELLI AND SON, RALPH ECOBELLI

Ecobelli's Tam O'Shanter: Superb Italian Cuisine

Dining out is always a pleasant experience, but dining out at **Ecobelli's Tam O'Shanter Inn is a gourmet's delight** . . . For here is the finest Italian cuisine in the area prepared with care by the Ecobelli family themselves . . . The atmosphere is warm and congenial. It was obvious that the guests were relaxed and enjoying the meal to the utmost . . . **My husband and I were greeted pleasantly and promptly escorted to our table by Anita, Ecobelli's gracious hostess** . . . We had a most difficult time deciding what to order since the menu is large and varied (there are five different scallopino dishes alone on the menu) . . . **We started our meal with a large antipasto which was a work of art to see**—Italian meats, olives, peppers, anchovies, egg wedges and assorted **vegetables on a bed of lettuce**—just scrumptious! . . . My husband chose Manicotti with meat balls and I had spaghetti with white clam sauce—both were superb . . . **After coffee and dessert we chatted with owner, Ralph Ecobelli**, and were given a "cook's tour" of the kitchen and banquet facilities and I must say that everything is **efficient, immaculate, and done in a professional manner** . . . Should your club or organization be planning a social affair, this would be a perfect spot . . . Ecobelli's of course, **serve a wide variety of American dishes in addition to their famous Italian cuisine** . . . There is a great source of pride taken by the Ecobelli family in the preparation, service, and enjoyment of their food . . . They want your dinner to be a delightful experience and **welcome your comments and compliments**. Do come out soon and pay them a visit . . . I'm sure you will find, as we did, that there is no finer Italian food in the area . . . **ECOBELLI'S TAM O'SHANTER INN**, Route 50, Ballston Spa, New York.

Before it even was a restaurant, the Tam received rave reviews from tavern customers who had discovered Laurina's food created in her small kitchen. The "word of mouth" reviews continued over the years, but it was a stellar recommendation by food critic Duncan Hines that put Ecobelli's on the map. Local newspapers provided good press too. However, it was the review by Gourmet magazine of which the Ecobelli's were most proud. The excerpt, above right, was reprinted for decades in the restaurant's menus.

Staff Memories

When we announced that we were creating this cookbook, we received comments and stories from some of the former staff at Ecobelli's, and were even able to visit with some of them. From what we learned, not only was the restaurant a great place to eat, it was also a wonderful place to work.
~ Lora Lee & Tom

I TOTALLY LOVED EATING all the great food at Ecobelli's and enjoyed working there, too! This was my first job, in the kitchen, bussing tables. Best pizza and spaghetti sauce! I remember when we'd pick up a party pizza and Janet Paquin would always give us little kids a lollypop. There are only great memories at Ecobelli's! I also have many, many childhood memories hanging around the barn near the restaurant with Goldie, Twinkle and Sparkle with Lora Lee, Tom and Donna — fun times! The restaurant is still up "For Sale" and I wish someone would buy it up — do a little redo, and it'd be perfect! ~ Claire Kindl Valentino

I JUST WANTED YOU TO KNOW I worked for your grams and your dad for almost 12 years. They were the greatest people I could know. Your family treated me as family. ~ Charlie Merchant

MY PARENTS VIRGINIA AND TONY FERRADINO brought us to "The Tam" at least once a week for the duration of our childhood and beyond. We spent every Christmas Eve there. Your grandmother Laura and your grandfather Dan were good friends and great people. After my freshman year at The College of Saint Rose, I was a waitress at the restaurant. That summer your grandfather was returning from Italy and we drove to New York to pick him up and bring him back to Ballston Spa. I earned more that summer waiting at the Tam than I was going to make in a year of teaching upon my graduation from Saint Rose in 1960. Your Dad was such a hard worker and nice to work for. I can't tell you how proud your Dad was of you. He and your mom, Mary, were so proud of you when you were born. In later years your Dad would tell me that when he visited you in New York City he met Arthur Miller who loved to come to your home for dinner, as you were a wonderful cook. Ralph said that he was so awed by being in the same room with him that he couldn't talk.

I was so fond of your Dad. He worked so hard in the kitchen and was always so good to me. One night a woman and her husband came in after the races. She had had so much to drink that she was abusive from the start. As you know, everything was cooked to order and she was obnoxious, complaining that her dinner was taking too long. When it finally was ready I went into the kitchen and put the dinners on the large round tray, lifted it up over my shoulder and the meals slipped off the tray and crashed onto the floor. I looked at your Dad and asked him what I should do. He told me to go out and tell them what had happened. It was the most difficult thing I have ever had to do. I went out and said, "You probably heard the crash in the kitchen. It was your dinners." She went ballistic and left. He never reprimanded me and helped me clean up the mess.

"The Tam" will always be a part of our childhood. My parents ran a dry-cleaning business and put in many hours, so we ate out a lot. We loved the food and we loved the atmosphere. I live in California now and my brother still lives in Ballston Spa, where he is a New York State Supreme Court judge. He spent many years as a Family Court judge prior to being elected to the Supreme Court. I am very interested in the movie that you are making and I'm sure that he will be also. Obviously we had no idea that Laura had been through so much. I just wanted to let you know that we remember. I often think about Anita [Stroebeck] and Bill Powers, and wonder what happened to them. There will never be another Italian restaurant with such an unlikely name. There will never be another "Tam." ~ Tonita Ferradino McKone

I WAITED ON TABLES AT ECOBELLI'S for several summers back in the early 60's. You could actually work your way through college then, and I would make $1,000 in tips in the summer and that $1,000 covered most of the tuition, room, board and expenses for the whole next year. We made great money.

People from New York City would show up each August. Laura would go crazy cooking special things for them. I recall walking into the kitchen one day and seeing a whole pot of calamari swimming in sauce, tentacles and all.

Your father Ralph dated my Aunt Hilda Aufiero before he was married, and Ralph also used to try to con me out of a portion of my tips based on the theory that without his work my tips wouldn't be as high!

Babs Schiavo was the bartender, much loved.

I expected to wait on tables for a fourth year, the summer before my last year in college. However, Sally Lawrence, who dated Joe Pepe, took my job. (I believe they got married and moved to Amsterdam.) Fortunately I got a job at the Trade Winds for that last summer. In fact, Lois, who worked at the Tam for years, also went to the Trade Winds and got me the job.

My favorite dish from the Tam was Chicken Romano. I hope you include that in your cookbook! The Tam had the best food in the tri-county area! ~ Sylvia Aufiero Matousek

BEST ITALIAN FOOD EVER, especially the sausage pizza. Janet [Paquin] sure knew how to make them. I worked in the kitchen and bussed tables through high school. Lots of good memories. ~ Richard Kindl

I HAD THE PRIVILEGE TO WORK for Laura, Dan and Ralph Ecobelli, starting when I was eighteen years old. I worked every summer for the five years when I would return home from college. Upon graduating from Plattsburgh, I became a teacher for the Ballston Spa Central School District, however I still would help them out on weekends and occasions such as New Years for a solid ten years.

They were the best people to work for, which helped to make it such a fun atmosphere; they treated and took care of myself and everyone as though we were family. I loved and miss them dearly.

Here are a couple of stories, which myself and others have shared over the last few decades. They will always be cherished moments for myself.

1) I was eighteen when Laura and Dan Ecobelli gave me the opportunity to serve as a waitress at The Tam. Everything went well the first week, as everyone was so kind and helpful. It wasn't until my second week that I would experience my first hiccup. It was a busy night and I was in the midst of picking up a few dinners when my tray, not balanced on the counter, crashed to the ground, losing four beautiful steak dinners. Needless to say, I was mortified and couldn't hold back the tears. I went down on my knees to start cleaning up the mess, all the while hoping that I wasn't going to lose my job, when two arms picked me up, turned me towards herself and said "Sweetie, now you are a real waitress." Laura kissed me on the cheek and said all will be okay. She was a warm and loving lady.

2) It was a busy night in August and two very happy couples had been waiting at the bar until their table was ready. It was apparent to everyone at the bar that they were having a great time, but as I went over to take their order they were in such good spirits that they decided to tell me all about how they were big winners at the Saratoga race track, were out celebrating, and would love another round of drinks. The group, after receiving their round of drinks, was seated at their table, where they thoroughly enjoyed their dinner and animated conversation. It was during dessert that one of the ladies called me over and asked me to help her husband who was about to be sick. I quickly took a handful of large white, cloth dinner napkins and made it over to him seconds before he got sick. I wrapped the napkins in a tablecloth, took them to the kitchen and tossed them in the dumbwaiter. Upon returning to the table to check on the gentleman, his wife pulled me close to her and whispered, "Honey, could you be a doll and check for us, we think my husband lost his false teeth when he got sick, but for as long as we've been drinking, we're not sure how long he's been missing them." Thankfully, I found the teeth, washed and returned them to a very grateful man. I certainly appreciated the very generous tip. ~ Susan Cinella Pupovac

PHYLLIS HOECK, ONE OF THE EARLY WAITRESSES at the restaurant, told me a great story about her years working there in the 50's. On her first day, Anita Stroebeck, the lead waitress, was put in charge of training Phyllis. Anita was a buxom and gregarious Swedish immigrant whom everyone loved. Phyllis was enamored of Anita. She thought she was very glamorous and strived to be just like her, with her upswept blond hair and dangly earrings. Anita was very talkative and had a signature laugh that brightened up the room. She knew every one of her customers by name and all of their life stories. With a twinkle in her eye, she explained that she had the male patrons wrapped around her fingers, the evidence of which was her bulging tip jar. The secret, she said, was that she never wrote anything down and explained to Phyllis that if she wanted to be truly great waitress, she had to memorize her customers' orders by heart. To be able to do that was quite a feat, especially during racing season when on the average each waitress serviced at least thirty tables a night. Anita was brilliant at memorization, always getting each order out perfectly. She did, however, like to imbibe quite frequently, having a shot or two with Babs the bartender, and by the end of the evening she was usually quite looped. You could always tell when Anita was knocking back a few because her loud contagious laughter rang throughout the restaurant. Despite that handicap she never once made a mistake.

So on Phyllis's first night she tried to emulate Anita's prowess at memorization. However, she wasn't prepared for it to be one of the busiest nights of the year. All went well until she forgot to include a few steak dinners on a customer's check. The customers went home happy but when Phyllis realized that she forgot to include the cost of their expensive meal on their bill, she was extremely distraught. She confessed to my father in tears, saying she wished she hadn't listened to Anita and had written her orders down, and then it would never have happened. She was sure she would be fired, but instead my father laughed and he told her not to worry, and it wasn't long before Phyllis mastered Anita's technique. The two waitresses soon became best friends and are responsible for helping the restaurant become famous for their efficient and friendly service.
~ Lora Lee

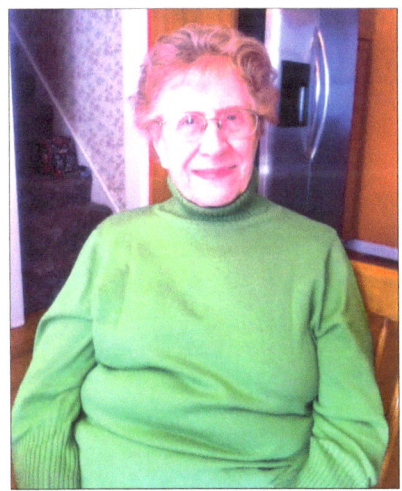

Phyllis in 2012

Word of Mouth

When we announced that we were creating this cookbook and asked for submissions from the public, we received an overwhelming response from friends and family. How nice it is to know that so many people have such great memories of the restaurant! ~ Lora Lee & Tom

THERE WAS NO BETTER PIZZA anywhere back in the day. Friendly staff and great food — many restaurants today could learn a bunch from your family's joint. Wish it was still around ~ Brien Hollowood

THANKS FOR THE MEMORIES of "over the river" as we would call it when we were upstate. ~ Louis Fischetti

THIS WAS THE BEST! And we could walk there! And go to the back door and get our pizzas … mmm … pizza … ~ Melissa Szeliga

I REMEMBER MY PARENTS going out there for anniversaries and our family buying great pizza there. And getting penny lollipops from there with Tommy and Sandy and Barbara. Great times! ~ Marie Brown

I REMEMBER GOING IN THE KITCHEN and coming out with delicious pizza! One time, when I was spending the night, I ate so much that my folks had to come get me early the next morning! It sure was good though. And let's not forget the eggplant parmesan. It was wonderful!
    I remember being in the Tam's kitchen with my dad. Your grandma and him were having a big discussion about sauces. Spoons came out and the tasting began. I'm not sure if it was over spaghetti or pizza sauce. I do remember standing there thinking, "Hey! I wanna taste!" ~ Michelle D'Elisiis

AWESOME pizza!!!! ~ Mark Dempsey

I LOVED THAT PLACE, especially the veal and peppers! ~ Holly Anderson O'Hern

MEATBALLS, Babs, munchies! ~ Susan Stomski Doherty

I JUST WISH I COULD FIND Italian sausage as good as the stuff on Ecobelli's pizzas. Almost 50 years and I can still remember the taste! ~ Karen Sorenson Lakey

YEARS AGO WHEN MY PARENTS were visiting New York with Laurina, she gave my father Tony a gravy ladle and to this day, every time I use it, my mom (Marie) reminds me where it came from! ~ Laura Weber

THE TAM … I loved going there. Thanks for the memories! ~ Joan D'Elisiis Hansen

I SPENT SO MANY ENJOYABLE times there. It was like Cheers — everybody knew your name. I remember the liquor decanters that went around the top of the dining room; Babs tending bar and Anita waiting on tables. The pizza from there is still compared to what we get today and is still considered the best pizza that was ever made. ~ Fran Capasso Dobroski

TOM — I'VE READ ABOUT YOU and your sister's involvement in honoring your grandmother by revisiting some of her recipes and her life. I grew up in Ballston Spa, and in our household every Friday night was spent at the Tam. My mother and father kept this up for probably 25 years.

I remember dearly Anita, Bill, Babs and Ralph as well as your grandfather. Your grandmother, of course, was the culinary expert, but I remember her most as a lovely lady. Of course it was easy for even a youngster like I was in those days to see how hard your grandmother worked. She made it look effortless and was always a sweetheart no matter how busy the restaurant got. Besides all of her fabulous Italian dishes (and I may have had them all at one time or another), the steaks and the lobster were also great. I live in the South now and I have to say I remember her Southern Fried Chicken as some of the best I've ever had.

The pizza was always the best and before I left town my father seemed to be stuck on Chicken Ecobelli. I must also say that Ralph was a phenomenon for the many years he worked in the kitchen and then ran the business when your grandmother got older. It was always obvious where he got his work ethic and talent from. Being a golfer I can attest that he didn't carry that talent onto the golf course, but he sure could cook!

Best of luck in all of your endeavors. As I'm sure you are well aware your grandmother was a remarkable woman. ~ John Hathorn

I RECALL AS A YOUTH in the '50s, being introduced to the "Pizza Pie." Our family made regular trips to The Tam, I have never tasted its unique flavor since it closed. The nearest I have come to it is a restaurant in Daytona Beach, Florida, called Genovese, very rare and distinct flavor. The atmosphere was elegant, as was the food. The bartender's name was Babs, and he was always dressed in black pants, starched white shirt and black bow tie offering a friendly greeting and quick service when one walked through the door. ~ Larry and Claire Dubois

WOW! I haven't heard the phrase "Tam O'Shanter" since I don't even know when! I grew up next door and ABSOLUTELY LOVED the aroma that came out of that place! Even as a kid, it always made me want pizza or spaghetti or whatever I thought of while smelling it! And every Halloween, Ralph (Mr. Ecobelli) would hand out lollipops to us kids! Great memories, great food! ~ Lisa Allen Stokely

OH, THE SIZE OF THE PLATE of spaghetti and meatballs was enormous! Of course I was so little that a dinner plate was twice my head! I'm going back to the 1960s and early '70s. Is that building still standing vacant? What a shame, it's been sitting there for so many years with no love brought inside. It needs a family to move into it and do whatever it is they love to do. ~ Suzie Dorsey

BEING THAT WE LIVED IN CARPENTERS ACRES behind the restaurant we could get the best pizza ever!! I remember going in the kitchen and waiting... Loving the aroma!!! Breaks my heart to see the place at a standstill. I make my lasagna like Tom C. taught my mom to do. Loved loved Ecobelli's! ~ Laurie Fenton Whalen

THE PIZZAS FROM ECOBELLI'S were the best. Every Friday night my parents would order us kids (Haskell's) pizza for supper. And I can remember the smells coming from the kitchen when picking up the pizza, and when we would ride our bikes around the parking lot. Wishing you guys all the best. ~ Joanne Mould

I JUST READ THROUGH A DRAFT of all the recipes in the Chickadee cookbook. What a wonderful cookbook. Scrumptious recipes that are not only a treasure trove of culinary delights, but of memories growing up in an Italian family. Thank you for sharing! ~ Patricia Bolgosano

THIS IS AMAZING! I am an immigrant myself and knew Mrs. Ecobelli personally when she used to order flowers and Christmas decorations for the restaurant. I had the first pizza ever at Ecobelli's. I still live in Ballston Spa. ~ Ingrid Voss-Melander

ECOBELLI'S WAS THE BEST Italian restaurant back in the day; only place I would eat meatballs other than my grandmother's, mother's or aunt's. One of the fond memories of my youth! ~ Mark Musto

OMG … I miss Ecobelli's pizza so much! So many memories of "kitchen" pick up! I can still smell the kitchen in my head! ~ JoAnn King Johnson

I WILL TURN 70 THIS SUMMER and I have many fond memories of Ecobelli's from childhood through just last month! I grew up in Jonesville and loved to hear my parents say we were going to "the Tam!" Often my dad would go in and bring out a pizza to the car and we would sit in the parking lot to eat it. On special occasions, we would dine in — often to be served by the waitress who never wrote any of the orders down! Kept everything in her head — including my favorite — spaghetti and meatballs! Babs was the lovable bartender who was "always" there! As an adult, I moved away from New York State, but, during visits back home (my 96- year- old mother still lives in the house), back to the restaurant I would go to visit with Babs, take out a pizza, eat free appetizers, and get my Ecobelli's fix! This was sometimes difficult during racing season as the regulars were, just that, regular! In recent years, after the restaurant closed, I would drive by hoping that it had reopened — to no avail! Ecobelli's and the Ecobelli family were long gone and I, and generations of others, are left with only our memories. Just last month, I drove by once more and stopped in the parking lot. The building's still there as are the memories! ~ Dave Knorowski

I WASN'T SURE if I was going to submit anything because … where do you start? My sister and I (Lesley Ryder — now Lesley Monaco) grew up with Lora Lee and Tommy Ecobelli. They lived next door to us on Route 50 just south of the village of Ballston Spa in an old farm house, and their grandmother and grandfather Laura and Dan Ecobelli lived next to them in a small brick house and then next to them was the Tam O'Shanter Restaurant. Then Lora Lee, Tommy and family moved into a newly built duplex on the other side of the restaurant. I'm not sure if they sold the farm house to the Hodgsons or if they rented to them because they still had a barn and pasture for Lora Lee's horse Goldie (a beautiful Palomino) and a cousin's horse named Duke. I used to take care of Goldie and Duke and also worked at Laura and Dan's house and also at the restaurant, after school and on weekends.

My mom Amy Ryder was the bookkeeper there for many years and was treated just like she was part of their family. All of the staff at the restaurant were treated like they were all part of one large family. Laura was a sweetheart — always thinking about everyone and always wanting to feed everyone. My mom was their bookkeeper for many years (late '60s into the '70s) until her health forced her to quit.

I can remember Thursdays was sauce day — that's when Laura would make her spaghetti sauce with sausage and veal in the sauce along with her meatballs! OMG! Her sauce was to die for! Laura also made lunch for everyone that was working in the restaurant during the day. She would make wonderful dishes like spaghetti and sauce, suffrites (delicious — chicken liver, kidney, onion, etc.) and great pizzas and sandwiches, etc. Laura always made sure her staff was fed and happy!

Poppsy (Dan Ecobelli) was usually overseeing the bar with "Babs" Schiavo until his health started to fail. His eyesight was failing and it was hard for him to navigate around the restaurant. I can remember when my mom came home one day and said Laura and Ralph taught her how to make the Roquefort dressing. She was happy about that because she loved that dressing on her salads and on veggies.

My sister, Lesley, worked at the restaurant (early- to mid-'70s) as a banquet worker (upstairs in the restaurant was a banquet room), and also checked coats. I worked for Laura and for Ralph ('69 to '74) doing odd jobs after school and on weekends — yard work and cleaning at Laura's home, cleaning at the restaurant, and also checking coats when the restaurant was open, and other odd jobs including some prepping of food. I also cleaned Goldie's stall (Lora Lee's horse) and groomed her and also exercised her. You had to be careful when riding Goldie because she would try and run your knees into the side of trees or the fence and would ocassionally try to rear up and throw you off! I can remember when she did that to Lora Lee and I think Lora Lee broke her collar bone that time. Ouch! Duke was a gelding that was also there at the barn who was owned by Lora Lee's cousin (I think, or uncle, I'm not sure) Tony D'Carlo and his daughter (I can't think of her name). I would also help out with his care when they were not around (they lived in the Amsterdam area). Laura and Dan were very kind and generous people.

Laura always made sure her staff was well fed and everyone was happy. She truly cared about the people that worked at the restaurant, and then when her health started to fail and Ralph (her son) took over the every day running of the business he also cared about his employees like they were family. In April of 1971 I can remember when my dad (Lester Ryder) and I were asked to go and get Laura and Dan from their winter home in Hollywood, Florida, and bring them back up to their summer home next to the Tam O'Shanter restaurant in Ballston Spa. I wasn't old enough yet for my license but I wish I could have driven — it was a little scary riding with my father down Interstate 95 doing 60 mph (fast for that time period)! I was reading the map (I was the co-pilot), but when the pilot doesn't pay any attention to the directions you are giving him it really is scary! Well, we did make it down and back and now I can chuckle about the experience.

I also remember all of the annual picnics that they would put on for their staff. It used to be at Kayadeross Park in Saratoga Springs (until that closed and became expensive condos), and then they were at the Saratoga State Park. The picnics were mostly put on by Ralph at that time because of Dan and Laura's health, and then after their passing away. I have many fond memories of the Ecobelli family — they were kind and generous and always made you feel like part of the family. I hope the movie and the cookbook does very well! If my mom was still alive she would have some great stories to add. ~ Greer Ryder Hotaling

I READ YOUR ARTICLE in the newspaper about the Ecobelli's Tam O'Shanter Restaurant and it brought back memories of when I was a young girl.

I can remember my father telling me about how he met your grandfather when he first came here from Italy and they became good friends. He was thinking about purchasing the restaurant but he was hesitant. My father, Tony DeSarbo, gave him encouragement and felt that it would be a good investment. Consequently, he did decide to purchase it and it became a very successful business venture.

That was our Sunday afternoon ride — from Schenectady to Ballston Spa — to enjoy our dinners at the restaurant. ~ Mrs. James Bachus

I HAVE LIVED IN BALLSTON SPA, New York all my life. Growing up in this village in the 1940's and 1950's everyone knew what a great place Ecobelli's Tam O Shanter was to dine in. Although I did not go there as a child, as a teenager I was able to become a patron. They had the best pizza, all homemade and fresh. The "Tam" was a place you went to to celebrate a special occasion. Be it a dinner for a birthday, anniversary or graduation, it was always highly regarded. When I married Paul Komar, a high school art teacher, we often would eat at least one dinner there per week. Before that, on the night before our wedding, we celebrated with all his relatives from Pennsylvania and Long Island at the "Tam". When our first child, Maria, was a little girl, Paul would take her there on Friday nights and they would order a pizza to go as I was now at home with her two younger brothers. Babs Schiavo would always fix Maria a Shirley Temple with the cherry on top. The area near the bar by the pizza pickup window always had some appetizers and Maria loved the miniature meatballs. She and her dad would bring some home to us. When I graduated from Russell Sage College in 1976, we had a family celebration there and when my mother, Helen Lynett, celebrated her 80th birthday, we were at the "Tam". Best wishes to the Ecobelli family in these endeavors. ~ Paul and Lorraine (Lynett) Komar

MY HUSBAND AND I are 88 years old and originally from Ballston Spa — my husband being born there. We now live in Agawam, Massachusetts. We have dined at Ecobelli's many times with my family. My two children were born in Ballston Spa. We left Ballston in 1955 but returned frequently as our roots were still there.

I do not recall too much about the bowling team as I was in my early twenties at the time. It was the latter part of the 1940's and the bowling alley was in Ballston Spa and I think it was "O'Brien's Bowling Alley".

As you are looking at the photo, I am the one in the middle with the vest reading "Tam-O-Shanter Inn." Looking at the photograph, first row: Laura Ecobelli; Mrs. Jordan (Madeline) Paddock; Mrs. Virginia Armstrong. Second row: Miss Dora Phillips; Mrs. Ralph (Mildred) Van Aernem; do not recall the third person's name. All the persons mentioned are deceased except me! ~ Madeline Paddock

TAKE-OUT MENU

ABOUT THE AUTHORS: LORA LEE ECOBELLI 0.98
ABOUT THE AUTHORS: TOM ECOBELLI 0.99
CHICKADEE: THE MOVIE 1.00

About the Authors

LORA LEE ECOBELLI

Lora Lee Ecobelli is an actress, writer, producer, director, singer-songwriter and teacher. Lora Lee's roles as an actress include Broadway and many Off-Broadway credits. She was the winner of the Harold Clurman Award for Best Leading Actress in an Off-Broadway Show for *The Vise*. Some of her favorite roles include: *A Christmas Carol, A Midsummer Night's Dream, Hamlet, Aurora Leigh, Fire Exit, The Trojan Women, Antigone, Hester Prynne at Death, Sea Island Nightmare, The Imaginary Cuckold, Lady of The Larkspur Lotion* and *The Little Oasis*. Her noted regional productions include *Blithe Spirit, On Golden Pond, The Three Sisters, The Seagull, Our Town, Lysistrata, Dancing at Lugnasa, A Street Car Named Desire, Spoon River Anthology* and *Talking With ...* .

Lora Lee's film and television credits include a leading role in the soon-to-be-released independent, *The Abolitionists*, as well as featured roles in *Judy Berlin, Carla, Jimmy's Cafe, Dose*, ABC's *Elmopalooza*, Comedy Central's *Upright Citizens Brigade* and MTV's *The Mom Song*. She is a proud member of AEA, SAG, AFTRA.

As a playwright, her plays have been widely produced regionally and in New York City. Several are published by Art Age Publications and Smith & Kraus. Her full length play *The Little Oasis* is featured in two anthologies by Smith & Kraus, *Best Women Monologues of 1998* and *Best American Scenes of 1998*. Lora Lee has since adapted *The Little Oasis* as a screenplay.

As a screenwriter, the feature film *Chickadee* was originally conceived and created by Lora Lee as a stage play. It enjoyed several successful New York productions before Lora Lee and her brother Tom Ecobelli decided to collaborate and develop it into a screenplay. *Chickadee* is based on their grandmother Laura Inzinna Ecobelli's 1922 journal, which tells the passionate story of the landmark trial in which she brought her abusive stepfather to justice.

Lora Lee also recently completed her first fiction novel, *Wanda-Allen*, and of course, *Laurina's Kitchen*, a family cookbook which she co-authored with her brother Tom.

As a singer-songwriter, Lora Lee has four CD's to her credit. Her music is diverse and eclectic, ranging from country to folk to jazz. She has performed both solo and with her band across the country at festivals and concert halls.

Lora Lee and her late husband Leo Burmester, along with actress Peggity Price, founded The Blue Horse Repertory Company. Blue Horse Rep is an exciting collage of professional actors, writers and musicians dedicated to the development of new works, as well as the performance of classics. Lora Lee and Peggity share the directing and producing responsibilities for the theater's many productions. Based at Arts on the Lake in New York's Hudson Valley, the blossoming theatre company is now branching out with satellite productions across the region. The company offers professional training programs for actors, taught by Lora Lee, with workshops for adults, children and people with special needs.

About the Authors

TOM ECOBELLI

Tom Ecobelli is an actor, writer and producer now based in the Los Angeles area. As an actor, Tom attended the American Academy of Dramatic Arts in New York and has performed in regional theatre, independent films, improvisational comedy, television sitcoms and national commercials. His notable credits as a guest star include the CBS sitcom, *Still Standing*, and Disney's *The Suite Life of Zack and Cody*.

Tom and his co-writer Heather George are producing *Animal Lovers Only*, an animal-driven feature that gives a behind-the-scenes look at emergency veterinary care, animal rescue organizations and animal shelters. Every animal "actor" used in the film will be taken from an animal shelter's death row and later adopted out to a loving home.

He and his co-writer Peter Marino's full-length comedy, *The Grandma Show*, has been produced numerous times in New York, Los Angeles and regionally. Tom and Peter have adapted it into a feature comedy screenplay as well. Tom's other play, *The Mouse*, written with Susan Touchbourne, was a finalist in the Edward Albee Theatre Conference in Valdez, Alaska. Another of their plays, *Slow Critters - Fast Food*, was produced in Los Angeles at First Stage Hollywood.

As a screenwriter, Tom has collaborated with his sister Lora Lee Ecobelli to develop her stage play into a screenplay, *Chickadee*. The script is based on the memoir of their grandmother, Laura Inzinna Ecobelli, written in 1922, which tells the passionate story of the landmark trial in which she brought her abusive stepfather to justice. He further collaborated with Lora Lee as co-author of *Laurina's Kitchen*.

Melissa Leo, Danny Glover and Paige Howard will star in Tom's feature drama, *Prairie Bones*, co-written with Susan Touchbourne, and directed by Connie Stevens. Tom is producing with Susan Touchbourne, Carolyn Long, and Concetta Di Matteo through their production company, IsWas (It Starts With a Story Productions).

Chickadee: the Movie

Laurina's Kitchen is a companion project meant to compliment Chickadee, our feature film based on a journal Laurina wrote as a young woman in 1922. Long before Ecobelli's was a reality, Laurina found herself at the center of a landmark child abuse trial. Although it was painful, she knew it was important to record what happened to her. Very few people knew what she endured as a child. When we were old enough she shared the journal with us. She expressed her desire to have her story told so that she could help other children overcome similar adversity and lead happy, healthy lives, free of the stigma and shame such tragedies can bring. Chickadee is our tribute to her and our attempt to help her dream come true. ~ Lora Lee & Tom

In a time when children's voices were silenced, Laurina, a courageous 13-year-old Italian girl, sparks a landmark, controversial trial when she accuses her stepfather of a shocking crime.

Two young Italian-American sisters, Laurina and Minnie, wait behind the gates of a Catholic orphanage for their immigrant mother Carmella. After their father died, Carmella was forced to leave them at the orphanage for years. Now remarried to Pietro, Carmella is finally able to bring her daughters home. Pietro charms everyone and the family looks forward to a new start.

With the help of his friend Vittorio, Pietro transplants the family to a farm in upstate New York, but their hopes for a new life are shattered when they're faced with the hardships of rural life and racial discrimination. Pietro rapidly declines. He forces Carmella and the girls to work long, grueling hours in a textile mill. What little money they do earn, he wastes on gambling and drinking. His condition worsens after he receives bad news from his father in Italy.

Laurina blossoms into a lovely young woman and slowly becomes the object of Pietro's obsession. At a mill-workers dance, Laurina shares her first innocent kiss with her date, Alberto. When the jealous Pietro finds out, he batters and sexually abuses her. Over the next several months he intimidates her into silence.

When Laurina becomes pregnant at 13, the truth can no longer be hidden. She makes the courageous decision to have Pietro arrested.

Laurina's strength and the ensuing influential, landmark trial unite the town and her family, lending inspiration to generations of silent victims.

For more information, visit the official movie web site at
www.ChickadeeTheMovie.com

Visit the *Laurina's Kitchen* web page to see
home movie clips of the Ecobelli family and
Ecobelli's Tam O'Shanter Inn
at

www.SquareCirclePress.com